NEW DIRECTIONS FOR STUDENT SERVICES

John H. Schuh, *Iowa State University*
EDITOR-IN-CHIEF

Elizabeth J. Whitt, *University of Iowa*
ASSOCIATE EDITOR

Strategies for Staff Development: Personal and Professional Education in the 21st Century

William A. Bryan
University of North Carolina at Wilmington

Robert A. Schwartz
Florida State University

EDITORS

Number 84, Winter 1998

JOSSEY-BASS PUBLISHERS
San Francisco

STRATEGIES FOR STAFF DEVELOPMENT: PERSONAL AND PROFESSIONAL
EDUCATION IN THE 21ST CENTURY
William A. Bryan, Robert A. Schwartz (eds.)
New Directions for Student Services, no. 84
John H. Schuh, Editor-in-Chief
Elizabeth J. Whitt, Associate Editor

Microfilm copies of issues and articles are available in 16mm and 35mm,
as well as microfiche in 105mm, through University Microfilms Inc., 300
North Zeeb Road, Ann Arbor, Michigan 48106–1346.

ISSN 0164-7970   ISBN 0-7879-4455-6

NEW DIRECTIONS FOR STUDENT SERVICES is part of The Jossey-Bass Higher
and Adult Education Series and is published quarterly by Jossey-Bass Inc.,
Publishers, 350 Sansome Street, San Francisco, California 94104–1342.
Periodicals postage paid at San Francisco, California, and at additional
mailing offices. Postmaster: Send address changes to New Directions for
Student Services, Jossey-Bass Inc., Publishers, 350 Sansome Street, San
Francisco, California 94104–1342.

New Directions for Student Services® is indexed in College Student Personnel Abstracts and Contents Pages in Education.

SUBSCRIPTIONS cost $56.00 for individuals and $99.00 for institutions,
agencies, and libraries. See ordering information page at end of book.

EDITORIAL CORRESPONDENCE should be sent to the Editor-in-Chief,
John H. Schuh, Campus Box 8, Wichita State University, Wichita, Kansas
67260-0008.

Cover photograph by Wernher Krutein/PHOTOVAULT © 1990.

Jossey-Bass Web address: www.josseybass.com

Printed in the United States of America on acid-free recycled paper con-
taining 100 percent recovered waste paper, of which at least 20 percent is
postconsumer waste.

CONTENTS

that they serve. It incorporates findings from a national survey of practitioner members of the National Association of Student Personnel Administrators (NASPA).

EDITORS' NOTES

Over the years, staff development has taken many forms in student affairs divisions and human resources departments across the country. As a new century approaches, the formulation of both personal and professional development strategies that meet the needs of student affairs staff in terms of management and support is imperative. Student affairs staff provide the human capital necessary for a wide range of student programs and activities in higher education. To effectively serve their campuses and students, student affairs staff must be provided with the necessary tools, resources, and learning opportunities to enhance their personal and professional growth. Clearly, the recruitment, retention, and development of staff are critical to the success of an organization.

For effective personal and professional growth of staff to occur, student affairs leaders must identify staff interests and needs to educate their staff in the delivery of quality service. The relationship between the personal and professional development of staff and accomplishment of the institutional mission is increasingly acknowledged by higher education leaders. Student affairs supervisors must make a strong commitment to a variety of learning opportunities to enhance skills, competencies, and knowledge in the ever-changing environment of contemporary higher education.

In the twenty-first century, an organization will not be successful unless employees are knowledgeable and committed to quality. Institutions of higher education must be good stewards of public funding and constantly strive for more efficient ways to do their work. Attention to the personal and professional development of staff is an essential first step in creating such a climate.

In Chapter One, Robert A. Schwartz and William A. Bryan explore the levels and types of professional development and expected outcomes. They set the stage for the discussion of personal and professional education and the main question, What is staff development?

An examination of performance-based human resource development (HRD) and its relevance for higher education and student affairs is presented in Chapter Two by Tyrone A. Holmes. Various practices such as human performance technology and human performance improvement are discussed, and strategies for application in student affairs are offered. The effective implementation of performance-based HRD in student affairs is demonstrated through discussion of a specific intervention.

In Chapter Three, Roger B. Winston, Jr., and Don G. Creamer argue that staff development in student affairs is best understood when viewed as an integrated staffing function closely bound to synergistic supervision and anchored in developmental career concepts. Synergistic supervision is a catalyst for the performance improvement of both the individual staff members and the institutional units. The authors present a taxonomy for conceptualizing and classifying goals that can help supervisors and staff design a balanced set of initiatives for improvement and venues for staff development both on and off campus.

New student affairs professionals, their supervisors and institutions, and the profession compose a team. The restrictions of limited resources and time and the absence of a shared philosophy can slow the potential of such a team. In Chapter Four, Patricia J. Harned and Michael C. Murphy consider these relationships and their impacts on new professionals. Special attention is given to developing the relationship between new professionals and their supervisors as an essential element for success.

In Chapter Five, Diane L. Cooper and Theodore K. Miller discuss findings from a national survey of practitioner members of the National Association of Student Personnel Administrators (NASPA). They explore the influence of mentoring on those entering and advancing in student affairs—the protégés—those providing professional development support—their mentors—and the organizations that they serve.

In Chapter Six, Joanne Nottingham examines the process of engaging student affairs professionals in reflective thinking. A three-dimensional view of professional development that focuses on personality, learning style, and behavior is discussed. Nottingham considers the importance of values, beliefs, ethics, attitudes, and life experiences as key factors in enhancing personal and professional performance.

Beverlyn Grace-Odeleye examines staff development program models from both historical and current perspectives in higher education in Chapter Seven. The Ball State University Division of Student Affairs staff development program model is discussed in detail. Recommendations and trends for the next century are presented.

Most educators acknowledge that there will be significant changes in the campus culture in the twenty-first century. In Chapter Eight, Bryan and Schwartz present an overview of the importance of staff development. Some significant staff development factors provided in various chapters are highlighted. Although there are many ingredients that go into the development and implementation of an effective staff development program, the authors focus on three important elements: the institution or division, the profession, and staff members.

William A. Bryan
Robert A. Schwartz
Editors

ROBERT A. SCHWARTZ is associate professor of higher education and student affairs at Florida State University. He has been active in higher education as a faculty member and administrator for twenty years.

WILLIAM A. BRYAN is professor emeritus of education in the Watson School of Education at the University of North Carolina at Wilmington. He served as a chief student affairs officer for eighteen years and is past president of the American College Personnel Association (ACPA) and the ACPA Educational Leadership Foundation. He has been actively involved in student affairs practice for thirty-seven years.

Staff development remains an elusive term in student affairs with a variety of meanings. In this sourcebook, development includes personal and professional education.

What Is Professional Development?

Robert A. Schwartz, William A. Bryan

In Homer's classic tale *The Odyssey*, Odysseus entrusted the care and training of his son, Telemachus, to his friend and confidant, Mentor. In the ancient world, it was essential for a father to train his son well in the areas necessary for success: hunting, soldiering, and, for an heir like Telemachus, how to work well with others and be a leader. To Odysseus, his son's education was so important that he sought the help of a person he could trust with his own life—his friend Mentor. Today, the term mentor continues to refer to a trusted relationship of guidance and advice.

A modern equivalent of Mentor can be seen in professional development. Much of our public life centers on professions. The act of mentoring is one of many activities clustered under a broader term, *professional development*. Many new professionals seek out mentors; however, their personal and professional development is influenced by many activities and opportunities during their career.

Like the guilds of the Middle Ages, many modern professions have a prescribed path of training and education. Carpenters, plumbers, masons, and electricians in contemporary society still follow strict guidelines for the development of critical skills in their professions. Specific career designations identify professional accomplishment and often serve as guidelines for wage and salary increases. These skill levels are governed by formal coursework, supervised apprenticeships or training, and, finally, by written examinations. A master plumber, for example, has usually spent *at least* seven years in the trade, first as an apprentice and then as a journeyman plumber. To become a master plumber, the journeyman must first meet the requisite training standards. Then he or she must pass a very difficult and extensive examination that requires skills and knowledge about fluid mechanics, chemistry, biology, engineering, and physics. Master plumbers are highly skilled, very experienced, and understandably highly paid.

Professions such as public accounting, law, medicine, and many others have similar training and education requirements. Many professions require continuing education and recertification or license renewal to maintain professional standing. Most professionals who work in student affairs are expected to have at least a graduate degree and to demonstrate related experience. New professionals in the field often serve apprenticeships of some sort in their graduate programs and continue to acquire new skills and training in their subsequent years of employment.

These early career experiences and the extensive training achieve several goals; they ensure a basic understanding of the language, history, traditions, symbols, and artifacts of a profession. In student affairs, graduate education provides common knowledge and understanding of a body of theory and practice across a diverse population. Through this educational process, new professionals become familiar with the field and acquire the basics of professional knowledge and skills. They also learn the expectations for professional standards of practice. As apprentices, new professionals are supervised by graduate faculty in graduate school and then by experienced staff early in their careers while they learn from personal experience.

Today, many of our current expectations for professional standards come from the standards developed by Abraham Flexner (1910) for medical education at the turn of the century. In the past, physicians typically were trained through apprenticeships and limited, proprietary education. Flexner set standards for professional training and education, including the expectation for formal education, professional standards, professional associations, ethics, and more. Other fields that emerged during and after Flexner have defined themselves by these same standards of professional education and practice.

Student Affairs

Although a relatively new profession, student affairs has a strong tradition of training and specialized education, as well. The early professional associations of deans of women (National Association of Deans of Women, founded in 1916) and deans of men (National Association of Deans of Men, founded in 1921) specified either graduate training and education or apprenticeships for new professionals eager to become deans (Schwartz, 1997). As those professional associations have grown over the years and more task-specific associations have developed in areas from financial aid to career services, each association has provided a new track of orientation and education for new professionals (Nuss, 1993).

A graduate degree is generally a prerequisite for new professionals in student affairs. Since the establishment of the first graduate program at Teachers College, Columbia University, in 1916, the demand for training has expanded to encompass over 100 graduate programs offering either master's- and/or doctoral-level training. Most position descriptions for full-time positions in student affairs and higher education administration include a graduate degree.

Despite these advances and high expectations, *professional training* and *professional development* remain elusive terms in student affairs. To define the concepts requires consensus about what is meant and expected when we say *professional development*. Other questions are, Who is responsible for the creation and execution of professional development opportunities within the field? Is it the institution, or are professional associations, like medieval guilds, responsible? Are graduate programs doing enough in their degree programs and general education requirements, or should a graduate student have more specific requisite skills in hand at graduation? To what degree is the individual responsible for his or her own professional development? If we can expect physicians, accountants, plumbers, and school teachers to maintain and advance their knowledge to renew a license or certification, should we expect the same of student affairs professionals?

Although this chapter does not answer these questions, it does attempt to generate discussion, thought, and more questions. There is no single correct point of view, or simple formula. The diverse nature of the profession of student affairs, the vast array of institutions, and the incredible variety of student affairs professionals demand a wide range of opportunities and possibilities for personal and professional development. This chapter sets the stage for the discussion of personal and professional education and the main question, What is staff development?

What Is Staff Development?

Staff development means something different to each person. In its most basic form it can be as simple as a plan to provide opportunities for staff to grow professionally or personally. As DeCoster and Brown suggest, "the need for continuous professional growth seems self-evident" (1991, p. 563). They suggest that personal and professional education is the goal of staff development.

Many definitions of staff development or professional development are outlined below. Taken from several authors, these illustrations exemplify the elusive nature of defining staff development, professional development, in-service education, staff training, and so on. Truitt (1969) defines in-service development as including "all activities engaged in by the personnel worker to improve the skills, techniques, and knowledge that will enable him to become an effective agent of education." The vehicles for in-service development include "workshops, formal courses, weekly or semiweekly staff meetings, discussions between student leaders and staff members, professional seminars, and attendance at national and state professional conferences" (p. 2).

Beeler (1977) claims that the term *staff development* "generally refers to in-service continuing education, or staff training, designed to enhance the competencies, skills and knowledge of individuals and to enable them to provide better services to their clientele" (p. 38). He argues that most divisions of student affairs do not give appropriate attention to establishing viable vehicles for the development of staff and that progressive organizations have ongoing staff development programs. Miller's research (1975) supports this observation. He states that at that time, "only one out of five institutions has formalized a policy statement about inservice staff development programming" (p. 262). Preston (1993) observes that despite strong agreement about the value of staff development programs, "implementation of such programs on a systematic basis in many institutions has not occurred" (p. 362).

Staff development programs should provide the opportunity for "general professional growth, refinement of existing skills, and acquisition of new skills to meet changing needs" (Canon, 1981, p. 447). These programs provide an active learning mode as "they increase knowledge, add to and enhance management skills and leadership techniques, broaden perspectives, and stimulate creativity" (McDade, 1987, p. iii). They can increase professional "knowledge, management and leadership skills, competency, creativity, credibility, job satisfaction, motivation, commitment, and job performance" (Bryan and Mullendore, 1990, p. 127). Merkle and Artman (1983) provide one of the most direct definitions of staff development: "a planned experience designed to change behavior and result in professional and/or personal growth and improved organizational effectiveness" (p. 55).

Staff development or personal and professional education programs should be at the heart of a student affairs division committed to quality. Instituting training and development activities and programs for management, support, and student staff should be a mandate rather than a choice. "All individuals working within a student affairs division should be included in the provision of programs and activities that meet needs for quality service and professional and personal growth" (Bryan, 1996, p. 11). Basic to a division of student affairs' pursuit of quality in serving students is the "development of programs and activities that improve staff work skills and further their understanding of vision and mission for an organization. . . . Further, staff should be encouraged and supported by leadership to be involved in continuing education and personal development programs" (p. 13).

Personal and professional education programs are delivered through many vehicles and provide opportunities for all staff (management, support, and student) to grow personally and professionally. These programs can meet personal needs of staff and help to accomplish divisional and institutional goals through staff skill development and improvement of skills. In addition, they can help staff enhance competencies and acquire new knowledge. Positive outcomes from these programs are competent, creative, motivated, committed staff providing quality services and a quality-driven organization effective in service to constituents.

Levels of Professional Development

Professional development can take many forms. Following are the levels likely to be common to most settings.

Individual. Many people are active in their own professional development. They may be taking advantage of tuition-deferred college or university courses in the pursuit of a degree or for personal enrichment. In a very broad definition, even a short course in keyboard skills or an aerobics course during lunch could be considered professional development. Participation in workshops offered by professional associations at regional or national conferences may be included, as well. Mentoring, by definition a relationship between two individuals, fits here, too.

Group or Program. One of the basic levels of organization in staff development is a cluster of individuals with a common interest or professional responsibility who come together to learn a new skill or to advance a professional interest. These individuals might participate in a workshop or attend a class together or form another type of affiliation out of common interest. The emphasis here comes from common individual interests, not necessarily a required or imposed expectation. Preston (1993) suggests that coffee hours can be developmental in nature, and certainly brown bag lunches on specific topics could be included as well.

Departmental. Much of the work in higher education is organized around specific work groups. The simplest organization is the department. For faculty, a department describes a loose confederation of semiautonomous individuals who may or may not share a common interest. In student affairs, a department more likely encompasses individuals working with each other daily on a common task such as financial aid.

When professional development concerns are addressed at the department level, they are likely to be confined to a job-specific issue or concern. To continue the financial aid example, a professional development goal within a department might be a workshop to explore new federal regulations for financial aid or counseling and advising skills to help department staff become more effective in working with clientele or in using new technology.

Divisional. Most student affairs programs are organized under a hierarchical structure with a vice president or dean at the top and departments or programs below. When program development is organized at the divisional level, it pulls together many people for a common purpose. A staff development program may be the result of a top-down decision by the vice president or dean, or it may be due to a committee decision by a group of individuals from across the division. It could even be directed by an outside person such as the college or university president.

This type of organizational effort may take the form of a large workshop or gathering, or it may take the form of a directive to be applied at lower levels of the organizational structure; for example, all departments will have a professional development plan. In either case, such a general program may not allow for individual interests or concerns because, by design, the effort is to affect the largest possible number of people. A divisional approach is important when specific information must be transmitted, such as training on a new computerized student database or an orientation program for all members of the division.

Professional Associations. Professional associations often provide opportunities for professional development at local, regional, and national meetings. As the Internet expands, professional associations are offering members listserves, discussion groups, and other forms of information sharing. Professional associations may be job specific and exclusive to specific interests, or they may be wide ranging and inclusive of most student affairs areas. Opportunities for new professionals, in particular, are often emphasized by professional associations. The greatest benefit of professional contact in an association comes with repeated personal contact and affiliation. The threshold experience of many new members in an association is to observe and slowly assimilate, which limits early involvement unless an activity is specific to new professionals.

The professional standards provided by the Council for the Advancement of Standards in Higher Education (CAS) (1997) represents the work of a wide range of student affairs associations. The council first developed standards for the practice of student affairs in the late 1980s. As a cooperative effort, the CAS standards cover a wide range of student affairs functions, directing both individuals and institutions in staffing levels, delivery of services, and ethical practices. Most important, CAS standards also address professional development and training, including graduate education.

Types of Professional Development: Formal, Nonformal, and Informal

To describe the types of professional development, three terms are borrowed from definitions created by the United Nations Educational, Scientific, and Cultural Organization (UNESCO) in the 1970s: formal, nonformal, and informal education. Formal education is, as it sounds, traditional classroom education with books, an instructor, and a set period. Nonformal education is "any organized, systematic, educational activity, carried on outside the framework of the formal system, to provide selected types of learning to a particular subgroup in the population" (Coombs, 1985, p. 23). Informal education can include learning in seminars, brown bag lunches, workshops, skill training—even adult literacy groups. Informal learning is learning by association and affiliation. Observation and imitation are clear examples; it is watching someone else do a task or job, or, more specifically (Bhola, 1983, p. 47), "the life long process by which every person acquires and accumulates knowledge, skills, attitudes, and insights from daily experiences and exposure to the environment." In fact, informal learning may be "unorganized, unsystematic and even unintentional at times, yet it accounts for the great bulk of any person's total lifetime learning—including that of even a highly 'schooled' person" (p. 24).

These terms make it possible to consider whether professional development is formal, informal, or nonformal. The distinctions can make a clear difference in who is involved, what is covered, and how to do it. Formal professional development is active, intentional training or education such as classes, specific workshops, or designed learning opportunities, often for credit or continuing education credit (CEU) or graduate study. Nonformal professional development may encompass many activities such as brown bag lunches, speakers, departmental training programs, orientation programs, professional association training and activities, and many more examples too numerous to mention here. Informal professional development includes observing, job shadowing, learning by example, and many mentoring activities discussed earlier.

Outcomes from Professional Development

Professional development is a term that appears frequently in primers and textbooks for graduate education in student affairs (Barr, Keating, and others, 1985; Delworth, Hanson, and others, 1989; Komives and Woodard, 1996) and in the general literature of the field. The professional associations, the American College Personnel Association (ACPA) and the National Association of Student Personnel Administrators (NASPA), discuss and describe professional development, as well. Although there is widespread agreement about the value of and need for professional development, there is less consensus on how to accomplish it.

Earlier descriptions explained levels (individual, department, divisional) and types (formal, nonformal, and informal) of professional development. Now we will focus on the delivery of professional development programs and activities. To remove some of the confusion about the motivations for and purposes of professional development, it is important to place professional development in the context of organizational theory.

Bergquist (1992) describes higher education as consisting of four cultures: collegial, managerial, developmental, and negotiation. The collegial and managerial cultures are the most familiar. A collegial culture describes faculty and others interacting as peers; the managerial culture describes a business perspective in which management stresses efficiency and performance. The negotiation model describes collective bargaining and politics. The developmental culture celebrates a humanistic belief in human values, positive change, and an emphasis on interdisciplinary functions, a contrast to the distinct boundaries of academic disciplines. In the developmental culture, Bergquist (1992) argues, teaching is valued over pure research; management is necessary but must respect the individual and the interpersonal domains.

Bolman and Deal (1991) use other organizational metaphors, including the symbolic culture and the organized anarchy of Cohen and March (1974) and Baldridge, Curtis, Ecker, and Riley (1978) to describe organizations. Bolman and Deal describe the symbolic culture through a metaphor of the "theatre" (p. 274). In the symbolic culture, the organization and its members "act" and strut the stage. In this culture, the importance of any event is not what happened, but what it means or how it is interpreted. Events have different meanings for many people, and many events are unpredictable. The more unpredictable events are, the harder they are to manage. In such an environment, people turn to symbols to provide meaning. Because events are more important for what they mean than what they do, the explanations provided by myths, rituals, and sagas allow us to interpret actions and offer acceptable and satisfying explanations for actions.

In each of these organizational cultures, professional development takes on many different forms. In a familiar culture, such as the collegial culture, professional development is an individual responsibility. In the managerial culture, a good manager assumes the paternal task of ensuring that professional development occurs and that employees participate. In a negotiation culture, professional development is a negotiated opportunity or right. In a developmental culture, enlightened leaders or managers may expect that individuals want staff development and help to provide it.

In the symbolic frame, professional development may be a ritual, a rite of passage, or a part of a larger process. Professional development is a symbol of how to achieve organizational mobility and progress. In a symbolic organization, a myth about professional development may encourage more participation and raise the level of interest. Rituals may even be associated with professional development activities—for example, certificates to reward those who have achieved new levels of learning or achievement—or it may be seen as a meaningless exercise or a rite of degradation, a symbol of inadequacy.

It is important for student affairs professionals and leaders to be clear in their own minds as to the purpose and direction of professional development in their institution and their sphere of responsibility. Is it to provide opportunities for advancement or expand existing skills? Is it critical to expand new skills and prior learning for new professionals? Consider the following excerpt from Barr and Associates (1993, pp. 349–350):

> We all have deficiencies in our academic training and preparation as we assume administrative positions in student affairs. The question becomes one of identifying what skills and competencies we must develop further, what knowledge we need to gain. Then we can design a plan to meet those requirements. . . . Staff salaries are by far the largest item in our budgets and our most important investment. It is essential that we assure that all professional and support staff members have the opportunity to refine their own skills to improve performance. . . . The commitment to improve professional skills and competencies rests, however, with each of us.

This statement on professional skills in student affairs represents several cultural perspectives (Bolman and Deal, 1991; Bergquist, 1992). The first sentence describes an environment that is collegial, developmental, and symbolic. The second sentence is much more in the context of the managerial culture, whereas the last sentence returns to the collegial and the symbolic.

Do these varied views make it difficult to incorporate professional development into practice? Of course. How is this conundrum resolved? As practitioners who believe in developmental theory and the developmental model, we want to believe in organizational change, development, and progress. These assumptions lead us to want to provide opportunities for growth for our colleagues, while, as students of organizations, we must recognize the symbolic nature of professional development activities. Emphasizing the need and the opportunity to expand knowledge, skills, and learning is important, but to require such activity by all staff becomes a very different proposition. Is such a requirement necessary? What is now being expressed both intentionally and symbolically? Whose time and energy are being controlled, and for what purpose? Occasionally, it may be necessary to impose a common training experience on all staff, such as using a new telephone system. In other cases, it may be critical, as Barr (1993) suggests, to provide opportunities for new professionals (and even mid- and late-career professionals) to address deficiencies or to keep abreast of rapid changes in the field.

Who should be included in professional development? Is it a measure of performance evaluation or merit? As Barr asks, just whose responsibility is professional development? Is it an individual responsibility or somewhat an organization's responsibility? Each of these questions is legitimate and worthwhile, and each must be considered carefully.

One benefit for all professionals is the transformative value of professional development. Whether it is achieved individually, in groups, in formal classes, or in a workshop, the process of renewal and growth essential for human development is more likely to be found in professional development activities than in any other activity. As we move into a new century, organizations are finding great value in the ability to change or transform quickly in response to new technologies, new opportunities, and new demands. These changes can come from outside the organization or from within.

Gouillart and Kelly describe the processes in *Transforming the Organization* (1995). They spend considerable time discussing the process of promoting growth and development for employees and explain that great organizations rely on more than just an elite few to manage. Great organizations know how to use people and their capabilities to their fullest extent, even creating second and third opportunities for those who may not quite have made it the first time but whose "values and intentions are in the right place" (p. 272).

Business and industry do not have the corner on the market when it comes to the development and application of new innovations in the management of people. Student affairs professionals should be able to apply the principles of human development and growth, simply by shifting the focus from students to staff and personnel. An example of such leadership is found in the story of Bob Shaffer, the legendary dean of students at Indiana University. During the campus turmoil of the 1960s and 1970s, Shaffer insisted that his staff join him on Saturdays for book discussions as a conscious effort toward staff development. Shaffer and staff were often out on campus until 2 a.m. and back at work by 8 a.m., so a Saturday commitment was not without sacrifice, but as Shaffer noted, "it was important to encourage people to grow . . . even if it meant we might lose some of them [to other jobs]" (Kuh and Coomes, 1986, p. 618).

Despite the constant uproar of campus protests and demonstrations, Shaffer, always the teacher, made time for himself and his staff to engage in lively, intellectual discussion to renew themselves and be better prepared for the next round of confrontation and dissent. Shaffer felt that his "most significant contribution was helping colleagues advance in the field professionally and develop personally" (Kuh and Coomes, 1986, p. 618). He was concerned about the resuscitation of an exhausted group of people, depleted not only physically but intellectually and spiritually. In this case, professional development becomes a source of renewal, a symbol of resilience, and an opportunity to develop intellectually, as well as professionally, and to remember the value of the university. Professional development can also be seen as an ethically responsible and necessary part of individual and organizational responsibility.

Concluding Comments

As professionals, we assume an ethical charge and duty to maintain a level of knowledge and currency in a chosen field (Bayles, 1981). Just as physicians or master plumbers are expected to be current in their knowledge of new research or improved practice, student affairs staff must accept their professional and ethical responsibility to stay abreast of change, as well.

Professional development may be the best means to achieve such growth and renewal. It may also be the only means to encourage and reward the development of staff at all levels. Colleges and universities are heavily dependent on human capital, so attention to and reinvestment in that capital, our most valuable resource, is time and money well spent. The worst choice is to ignore or overlook professional development. In the following chapters, the issues and questions raised in this chapter are examined in greater detail.

References

Baldridge, J. V., Curtis, D. V., Ecker, G., and Riley, G. L. *Policy Making and Effective Leadership*. San Francisco: Jossey-Bass, 1978.

Barr, M. J. "Introduction to Part Four: Acquiring and Developing Administrative Skills." In M. J. Barr and Associates, *The Handbook of Student Affairs Administration*. San Francisco: Jossey-Bass, 1993.

Barr, M. J., and Associates. *The Handbook of Student Affairs Administration*. San Francisco: Jossey-Bass, 1993.

Barr, M. J., Keating, L. A., and Associates. *Developing Effective Student Services Programs: Systematic Approaches for Practitioners*. San Francisco: Jossey-Bass, 1985.

Bayles, M. D. *Professional Ethics*. Belmont, Calif.: Wadsworth, 1981.

Beeler, K. D. "Mini-U: A Promising Model for Student Affairs Staff Development." *NASPA Journal*, 1977, 14 (3), 38–43.

Bergquist, W. H. *The Four Cultures of the Academy: Insights and Strategies for Improving Leadership in Collegiate Organizations*. San Francisco: Jossey-Bass, 1992.

Bhola, H. S. "Non-Formal Education in Perspective." *Prospects*, 1983, 13 (1), 45–53.

Bolman, L. G., and Deal, T. E. *Reframing Organizations: Artistry, Choice, and Leadership*. San Francisco: Jossey-Bass, 1991.

Bryan, W. A. "What Is Total Quality Management?" In W. A. Bryan (ed.), *Total Quality Management: Applying Its Principles to Student Affairs*. New Directions for Student Services, no. 76. San Francisco: Jossey-Bass, 1996.

Bryan, W. A., and Mullendore, R. H. "Professional Development Strategies." In R. B. Young, *The Invisible Leaders*. Washington, D.C.: National Association of Student Personnel Administrators, 1990.

Canon, H. J. "Developing Staff Potential." In U. Delworth, G. R. Hanson, and Associates, *Student Services: A Handbook for the Profession*. San Francisco: Jossey-Bass, 1981.

Cohen, M., and March, J. G. *Leadership and Ambiguity*. New York: McGraw-Hill, 1974.

Coombs, P. H. *The World Crisis in Education: The View from the Eighties*. New York: Oxford University Press, 1985.

Council for the Advancement of Standards in Higher Education. *CAS: The Book of Professional Standards for Higher Education*. Washington, D.C.: Council for the Advancement of Standards in Higher Education, 1997.

DeCoster, D. A., and Brown, S. S. "Staff Development: Personal and Professional Education." In T. K. Miller and R. B. Winston, Jr., *Administration and Leadership in Student Affairs: Actualizing Student Development in Higher Education*. Muncie, Ind.: Accelerated Development, 1991.

Delworth, U., Hanson, G. R., and Associates. *Student Services: A Handbook for the Profession*. (2nd ed.) San Francisco: Jossey-Bass, 1989.

Flexner, A. *Medical Education in the United States and Canada*. Bulletin no. 4. New York: Carnegie Foundation, 1910.

Gouillart, F. J., and Kelly, J. N. *Transforming the Organization*. New York: McGraw-Hill, 1995.

Komives, S., and Woodard, D. *Student Services: A Handbook for the Profession*. (3rd ed.) San Francisco: Jossey-Bass, 1996.

Kuh, G. D., and Coomes, M. "Robert H. Shaffer: The Quintessential Do-Gooder." *Journal of Counseling and Development,*1986, 64, 614–623.

McDade, S. A. *Higher Education Leadership*. Washington, D.C.: Clearinghouse on Higher Education, The George Washington University, Association for the Study of Higher Education, 1987.

Merkle, H. B., and Artman, R. B. "Staff Development: A Systematic Process for Student Affairs Leaders." *NASPA Journal*, 1983, 21 (1), 55–63.

Miller, T. K. "Staff Development Activities in Student Affairs Programs." *Journal of College Student Personnel,* 1975, 16 (4), 258–264.

Nuss, E. M. "The Role of Professional Associations." In M. J. Barr and Associates, *The Handbook of Student Affairs Administration*. San Francisco: Jossey-Bass, 1993.

Preston, F. R. "Creating Effective Staff Development Programs." In M. J. Barr and Associates, *The Handbook of Student Affairs Administration*. San Francisco: Jossey-Bass, 1993.

Schwartz, R. A. "Reconceptualizing the Leadership Roles of Women in Higher Education: A Brief History on the Importance of Deans of Women. *Journal of Higher Education,* 1997, 68 (5), 502–522.

Truitt, J. W. *Factors Underlying the Need for In-Service Development Programs in Student Personnel Work*. East Lansing, Mich.: National Center for Research on Teacher Learning, 1969. (ERIC Document Reproduction Service no. ED 022 203)

ROBERT A. SCHWARTZ is associate professor of higher education and student affairs at Florida State University. He has been active in higher education as a faculty member and administrator for over twenty years.

WILLIAM A. BRYAN is professor emeritus of education in the Watson School of Education at the University of North Carolina at Wilmington. He served as a chief student affairs officer for eighteen years and is past president of the American College Personnel Association (ACPA) and the ACPA Educational Leadership Foundation. He has been actively involved in student affairs practice for thirty-seven years.

Human resource development holds great promise for twenty-first-century student affairs professionals.

Performance-Based Approaches to Human Resource Development

Tyrone A. Holmes

Over the years, much has been written about the practice of human resource development (HRD) and its growing impact on the nation. Training and development have flourished as professional functions and are now used in a variety of organizations. Between 1983 and 1991, training activities increased nationally by 45 percent (Carnevale and Carnevale, 1994). Businesses, government agencies, and educational institutions spend billions of dollars each year on employee development and education. The Bureau of Labor Statistics estimates that U.S. organizations spent a total of $55.3 billion on training in 1995 alone. The national Human Performance Practices Survey suggests a similar training expenditure for 1996 (Bassi and Van Buren, 1998).

Recent literature, however, points to significant concerns with current HRD practices. Galagan (1994) emphasizes that training and development, in their current forms, run the risk of obsolescence because they fail to focus on the enhancement of individual and organizational performance. Rothwell (1996) agrees that training must directly influence this goal if it is to remain useful for organizations.

This chapter examines performance-based human resource development practices and their relevance in student affairs. The following section provides a general overview of HRD, including discussion of the newest concepts in the field, such as human performance technology and human performance improvement. The rest of the chapter offers a model and tools for performance-based HRD in higher education and student affairs and relates a specific example of effective implementation.

The Practice of Human Resource Development

Human resource development is a systematic process that includes training and development, organization development, and career development to enhance individual, group, and organizational effectiveness. It emphasizes the integrated application of these components to engender higher levels of individual and organizational effectiveness than would occur if a narrower approach were applied (McLagan, 1989).

Training and Development. Training and development help individuals gain key workplace competencies to meet the requirements for current or future jobs. The main emphasis of training and development is on individuals and their primary work roles. Most training and development outcomes are achieved through individualized learning such as training workshops, coaching, or on-the-job learning (McLagan, 1989).

Organization Development (OD). Organization development is a planned process of organizational change that is designed to benefit both individuals and organizations. The primary emphasis of OD is to improve relationships and processes among individuals and groups so that work is distributed more effectively. OD goals are met through organizational processes such as team development and process improvement initiatives (Coyne, 1991; McLagan, 1989).

Career Development. Career development is a systematic approach to ensure that each individual's interests, values, and skills are effectively aligned with the organization's workforce requirements. It is a process by which individuals plan their careers in connection with an organization's strategic direction. The primary emphasis of career development is on the individual. Positive outcomes are achieved by improving one's knowledge about a career field and by influencing the organization to create optimal matches between individuals and their work roles (Gutteridge, Leibowitz, and Shore, 1993; McLagan, 1989).

Human Performance Technology

Human performance technology (HPT) is an analytical process that links organizational strategy and goals to an individual's ability to achieve them through a variety of systematic interventions. Such interventions often include training and development, organization development, and career development. HPT provides methods for solving problems and identifying opportunities related to individual performance. The ultimate goal is the improvement of human performance in ways that positively influence institutional goal attainment (Bricker, 1992; Callahan, 1997; Rothwell, 1996; Stolovitch and Keeps, 1992). Human performance technology is a new discipline that emerged from the confluence of principles offered by several distinct fields including systems theory, behavioral and cognitive psychology, instructional systems development, and human performance analysis (Rothwell, 1996; Stolovitch and Keeps, 1992).

Human performance theory adopts a systems view of organizations that recognizes the interrelatedness of an organization's subsystems and seeks to link all of the actions that affect total performance. For instance, an HPT approach to enhancing performance would certainly include examination of an organization's human resource development function, but it would do so along with other functions such as recruitment, selection, orientation, compensation, and performance management. These functional areas are part of an organization's human performance system (HPS). Such a system represents the comprehensive and integrated design of a standard human resource function. Its purpose is to directly support the achievement of institutional objectives while simultaneously developing top professionals. Other components in an organizational human performance system might include career planning and development, outplacement, diversity management, work practices and processes, and various technologies (Mone and Bilger, 1995).

A well-developed human performance system helps an organization create a high-performance work system (HPWS) that describes specific patterns of work structures, practices, and processes and consists of many interrelated parts that operate synergistically to achieve institutional goals. The parts include components of the human performance system, as well as the organization's strategy, vision, mission and goals, core values, and management practices. To create a high-performance work system, an organization must consider how its work gets done and then design the most effective and efficient system possible to achieve its goals. Because most organizations significantly rely on humans to perform work, the HPS, and the development of the people within it, becomes vital (Gephart and Van Buren, 1996).

Human performance technology is grounded in behavioral and cognitive psychology. These academic disciplines provide a theoretical basis for the facilitation of learning. This theoretical background, along with principles from instructional systems development, allows the HPT practitioner to design interventions that cultivate learning for organizational members and to do so in ways that improve institutional effectiveness (Rothwell, 1996; Stolovitch and Keeps, 1992).

The hallmark of any HPT intervention is the systematic analysis of human performance and the diagnosis of performance problems within the organization. Through use of this process human performance technology can help organizations achieve the ultimate goal of human performance improvement (HPI). Human performance analysis and improvement typically involve several stages including problem definition, cause analysis, intervention planning, implementation and change management, and evaluation, as described next.

Problem Definition. During the problem definition stage, the organization attempts to identify performance problems and opportunities, such as identifying exemplary performance and making comparisons with current levels of performance. This process allows the institution to detect where the performance gap is and to identify the specific performance areas that can be improved. It also helps identify who is most affected by the performance gap, to learn when the gap first occurred, and to clarify its effects on the organization.

Cause Analysis. Cause analysis is the systematic identification of the reasons for performance problems. It helps an organization determine the causes for poor performance and to find out why certain problems occur. During this stage a variety of diagnostic tools is used to simplify the performance analysis process. Such tools might include force field analysis, competency models, the fishbone diagram, and the human performance improvement worksheet, which are discussed later in this chapter.

Intervention Planning. During the intervention-planning stage, organizations make decisions about how they will address performance problems and take advantage of performance opportunities. They identify the specific interventions needed to close performance gaps by addressing their underlying causes. It is also during this stage that the institution identifies the specific objectives of the intervention, and it then bases all activities on these objectives.

Implementation and Change Management. After an intervention plan is developed, participants must simultaneously implement the plan while facilitating the organizational change process. The plan involves several activities, including observing the extent to which the intervention is addressing the underlying causes of the performance gaps, identifying measurable improvements, and helping organizational members to better understand the purpose of the initiative and the role they play in its success. It is particularly important to ensure that key members of the organization show support for the performance improvement intervention (Rothwell, 1996).

Evaluation. Finally, during the evaluation stage, the organization must formally assess the extent to which intervention objectives were achieved and performance gaps have closed. The human performance technologist considers other issues, as well, during this stage. These include examination of positive and negative side effects, the extent to which the intervention has been assimilated into organizational culture, and the lessons learned that can be applied in future initiatives (Rothwell, 1996).

The Shift from HRD to HPT

Although significantly related and obviously interconnected, human performance technology departs from traditional human resource development along several philosophical lines. Gill (1995) describes the paradigmatic differences between training and HPT. He identifies five myths regarding the practice of human resource development that tend to limit its effectiveness in today's organizations. These myths involve faulty beliefs such as the belief that training, on its own, will make significant differences in individual and organizational performance; that the primary purpose of training is to achieve learning objectives; that the trainer's primary purpose is to manage training program facilitation; that ultimately, training is the training department's job; and that participants should enjoy the training experience.

This limited view is based on the notion that HRD is in the business of training. Training alone is not always the key to effective staff development, solving organizational problems, and improving human performance. HPT acknowledges the vital role training must play in organizations, but it emphasizes learning that is directly related to individual and organizational performance. The HRD model also supports the notion that training is a program with a finite beginning and end. It looks for quick fixes to deep-seated institutional problems that often require more synergistic and systematic solutions. It seeks immediate results over the short term and often compartmentalizes organizational functions during this process (Gill, 1995).

Conversely, the HPT paradigm assumes that training and development are often insufficient to effectively resolve problems or to enhance institutional performance. It recognizes that there are no quick fixes and that significant problems require analytically based solutions, solutions that are often achieved by taking the long-term view of organizational change and by the systematic integration of organizational functions (Gill, 1995).

The recent movement from traditional human resource development to HPT has brought with it a host of philosophical and organizational changes, most notably the creation of learning environments. Environments are designed to shift learning from isolated skill development and information transfer to performance improvement. Likewise, learning environments shift the educational focus from the teacher to the learner by increasing self-directed and team-based learning and by maximizing the use of various educational technologies (Galagan, 1994).

These changes have ushered in new roles for performance-based human resource development practitioners. These new roles are based primarily on linking training activities and outcomes to organizational needs and goals, maintaining a strong customer focus in the development of new educational initiatives, using a systems view of performance, using various tools and processes to effect desired outcomes within the organization, and evaluating the outcomes of training in relation to its impact on individual and organizational performance (Gill, 1995).

Human Performance Technology and Student Affairs

The question remains, Is human performance technology a relevant tool for student affairs departments? The answer is yes for several reasons. Many authors have written about the importance of staff development in student affairs (DeCoster and Brown, 1991; Preston, 1993), which can only deliver quality programs and services to the extent that they have highly skilled professionals. Some authors suggest that current development efforts are inadequate (Preston, 1993). Human performance technology, with its dual emphasis on professional development and organizational improvement, can fill this void.

Higher education institutions are extremely complex organizations. Birnbaum (1991) characterizes them as "organized anarchies" (p. 153) composed of shifting coalitions that bargain for desired outcomes, outcomes that may not be universally shared or endorsed. HPT, with its strong focus on systems analysis and intervention, offers the opportunity to bring order to these complex systems in ways that can enhance both individual development and organizational performance. Similarly, higher education institutions are grounded in a philosophy of teaching, learning, and human development.

One of the primary missions of student affairs is the facilitation of student learning and development. The American College Personnel Association's Student Learning Imperative (1994) emphasizes the primacy of the student affairs role in this arena; it states that student affairs practitioners share educational responsibilities with faculty and are responsible for creating the conditions under which student learning is likely to occur. The creation of learning environments is well aligned with the philosophy and practices espoused by human performance technology. Because HPT is grounded in systems theory, cognitive and behavioral psychology, instructional systems development, and the creation of learning-centered organizations, it has great confluence with the student affairs mission.

Performance-based human resource development can be very useful in student affairs departments. For this to happen, however, student affairs must make effective and efficient use of human performance technology. This goal can be achieved by adhering to five basic tenets:

- Staff development activities in student affairs should be systematically geared toward enhancing development in ways that influence the attainment of specific objectives and the creation of high-performance work systems.
- This goal can be achieved by applying human performance technology tools and processes.
- The tools and processes used must be based on a careful analysis of organizational needs and structures.
- The process of creating a work system can be maximized by the development and implementation of a high-quality human performance system in student affairs.
- Development of the human performance system should be the primary focus of initial efforts in performance-based human resource development.

A Human Performance Systems Model for Student Affairs

Development of an effective, integrated human performance system offers several benefits to student affairs organizations. First, it provides a foundation for the continuous and appropriate development of all student affairs professionals. Second, it helps the group create a greater sense of community within the organization. Finally, and perhaps most importantly, it provides a methodology, along with the various HPT tools and processes, for student affairs practitioners to effectively unite professional development and organizational effectiveness.

To obtain the greatest benefits from the human performance system, the following components should be considered in the student affairs department.

Recruitment, Selection, and Retention. This effort includes all of the activities that are associated with identifying potential professional staff candidates, identifying the candidates who are the best fit for both the job and the institution, and providing systems and activities geared toward ensuring that staff members stay in the organization. The focus here is on the design and implementation of an effective and efficient process that brings a diverse group of high-level performers into the student affairs department.

Performance Planning and Goal Setting. The first step in the performance management process is the collaborative identification of employee goals and objectives. This process includes setting performance goals, planning how these goals can most effectively be accomplished, and ensuring that each professional staff member is engaged in activities that will ultimately help the division achieve its objectives.

Performance Coaching. When performance plans and objectives have been identified, student affairs administrators must engage in a continuous process of leading and motivating their staff members. Effective coaching allows supervisors and their employees to build stronger relationships and to work together to attain employee performance goals. It is also a very effective way to help the student affairs professional staff to develop, to receive positive and constructive feedback, and to play an empowered and informed role in the execution of their job responsibilities.

Performance Assessment. Most organizations require some type of performance appraisal process. This process is necessary to establish and maintain the conditions required for effective performance management. When properly facilitated, performance assessment confirms employee understanding of work roles, evaluates the extent to which performance goals are being met, identifies problems and barriers in the work environment, provides both positive and constructive feedback, encourages regular job-related conversations between supervisors and employees, and provides the information needed for the performance reward process (Brennan, 1989).

Performance Reward. Compensation systems must be aligned with organizational goals and facilitate staff development. The performance reward process consists of the allocation of employees' salary and benefits. When effectively implemented, the reward system provides specific consequences for actual performance and feedback concerning the merit of these accomplishments (Brennan, 1989).

Employee Development. Employee development includes all activities that directly or indirectly influence the ability of the student affairs professional to do his or her current or future job. This process requires identifying the competencies needed to effectively perform one's job and ensuring that development activities are geared toward enhancing those competencies. Employee development can take many forms in student affairs, including attending professional conferences, on-the-job training, new employee orientation, on-site workshops and programs, formal classroom education, training programs offered thorough the college's HRD office, computer-based training, and self-study activities.

Career Planning and Development. Career planning in student affairs consists of the systematic approaches used to ensure that each staff member's interests, values, and skills find confluence with the department's workforce requirements and needs. For the staff member, a high degree of fit can lead to increased job satisfaction, commitment, and competence. For the student affairs department, enhancing the fit between the individual and the institution can lead to higher levels of performance and productivity. Career development in student affairs can include a variety of activities such as tuition reimbursement, career-planning workshops and seminars, staff orientation programs, job posting, individual and group counseling, career coaching, job enrichment, and release time to take graduate courses.

Career Transition. It is inevitable that some staff members will leave the organization, either voluntarily or involuntarily, because of changing institutional needs; interest, value, or skill mismatches; or limited career opportunities. An important component of the human performance system is a process for making this transition smoothly. Ideally, staff members who leave the institution will have the skills and knowledge necessary to make a seamless transition into gratifying work outside the organization.

Organization Development. The primary focus of organization development (OD) in student affairs is on a planned implementation of organizational changes that benefit students, staff members, and the institution as a whole. Such changes are geared toward improving relationships and processes among individuals and groups so that work processes can be facilitated more effectively and efficiently. The main goal of any organization development intervention is to create systems that enhance the ability of student affairs practitioners to do their jobs. OD interventions in the student affairs department might include creating self-directed work teams, team development, total quality management, business process reengineering, process consultation, and survey research.

Diversity Empowerment. Diversity can be defined as "the mosaic of people who bring a variety of backgrounds, styles, perspectives, values and beliefs as assets to the groups and organizations with which they interact" (Rasmussen, 1996, p. 274). Diversity empowerment provides the philosophical foundation for the entire human performance system. It is an intentional, proactive approach to creating an environment in which members accept, respect, celebrate, and effectively use the diversity within an organization as a source of added value. As such, the environment should fully support the benefits of diversity within communities and organizations, include members of diverse social groups as full participants, reflect the contributions and interests of these diverse constituencies, and act to eradicate all forms of social injustice.

Human Performance Technology Tools for Student Affairs

Several HPT tools are of particular relevance for student affairs. These tools can help enhance the professional development of both students and professional staff, and they are specifically oriented toward enhancing individual and organizational performance.

Competency Modeling. Competency modeling, a very popular human performance technology tool, is a systematic process designed to identify the skills, knowledge, abilities, and attributes needed for high performance in a particular position. Competencies are the characteristics associated with high performance within a specific job. These can include task competencies, result competencies, output competencies, and knowledge, skill, and attitude competencies (McLagan, 1997). The competency model itself is the result of analyses that differentiate high-level performers from average and low performers (Mirabile, 1997).

The competency modeling process involves several steps, which are designed to position the competency program as a major organization development intervention within the institution. They include understanding how institutional work processes have changed and will continue to evolve over time; identifying the specific competencies required to carry out the work processes in this new environment at high levels of performance; assessing the knowledge, skills, and abilities of current staff members in each of these competency areas; comparing staff members' current levels of knowledge, skills, and abilities with desired competencies and identifying the gaps; and setting up developmental interventions designed to close these gaps and enhance the competency levels of current staff members (Fox, Kennedy, and Vitale, 1997).

Force Field Analysis. Another popular HPT tool is force field analysis (FFA). Force field analysis is an analytical process designed to help examine the dynamics of a problem situation. It is based on the idea that any problem, goal, or need is balanced by two forces: driving forces and restraining forces. Driving forces are the forces that facilitate positive change such as accomplishment of a goal, resolution of a problem, or fulfillment of a need. Restraining forces inhibit positive change. They include the forces that prevent goal achievement, problem resolution, and need fulfillment (Eitington, 1989).

Force field analysis can be used for performance-based human resource development in student affairs. For example, this technique can be used by identifying staff performance level as the problem to be analyzed within the FFA model. If there is a performance problem in a student affairs unit, the problem can be analyzed by identifying the driving forces that might lead to desired levels of performance and the restraining forces that currently inhibit attainment of this performance level. By specifically identifying key driving or restraining forces, staff members can better understand how to most effectively facilitate positive performance in a variety of areas.

Cause-and-Effect Diagram. Rothwell (1996) emphasizes the utility of another HPT tool, the cause-and-effect diagram. Also known as the fishbone diagram because of the way it is shaped, it is often applied during the "cause analysis" stage of the human performance improvement process. The cause-and-effect diagram is designed to help performance technologists identify the specific causes of human performance gaps. The power of the fishbone diagram lies in its ability to vividly display the relationship between some effect (for example, a performance problem) and its probable causes.

The fishbone diagram is typically used during a brainstorming session of a team or group. Group members work together to identify desired performance outcomes and to decide what is happening in a given situation; then, they seek to identify the possible reasons for this gap.

Human Performance Improvement Worksheet. A final HPT tool that can be effectively applied in student affairs is the human performance improvement worksheet (Holmes, 1997). This worksheet, developed by the author, helps organizational members identify performance problems and isolate the reasons that the problems exist. It is based on the notion that the causes of any employee performance problems can be classified into one or more of five categories: (1) employees do not know what is expected of them (communication problem), (2) employees do not know how to do what is expected of them (training problem), (3) employees do not want to do what is expected of them (motivation problem), (4) employees just cannot do what is expected of them (selection problem), or (5) barriers prevent employees from doing what is expected of them (organization problem).

For a given performance problem, student affairs staff members can use the human performance improvement worksheet to specifically identify the underlying causes. Based on these causes, effective interventions (for example, training and development, improved hiring practices, removal of organizational barriers) can then be designed and implemented to help performance improvement in the desired areas.

Applying Human Performance Technology to Student Affairs

One way that student affairs departments can immediately use human performance technology is through the application of HPT tools to facilitate the performance improvement process. The following example represents an actual case of applying the competency modeling process to staff development in the college of engineering at a major Midwest university.

The Situation. A large department within the college of engineering was interested in improving the performance of its management team. This team was composed of five professional staff members who were responsible for managing all aspects of a major summer engineering program involving hundreds of students. These processes included hiring, orienting, training, supervising, and evaluating both professional and student staff members.

The director of this department wanted to ensure that each management team member had the skills, knowledge, and abilities needed to function at the highest levels of performance. A competency model process was implemented because of its ability to identify the skills and attributes needed for high performance in a particular position.

The Process. There were three primary goals for the competency modeling process. These included identifying key skill or knowledge sets, ranking the primary competency need areas, and carrying out management team development activities based on the results of the competency model. There were several key steps in this competency model approach. The first step involved identifying the staff members who should be directly involved in the process. The consultants decided to include the five management team members themselves, their direct supervisor, and six of their employees. This process allowed for many perspectives and opinions regarding the management team's current level of functioning.

The next step involved describing the purpose and process of competency modeling to participants. It was important for them to understand why consultants were doing this evaluation, the step-by-step process involved, and the outcomes that could be expected. After clarifying the purpose and process to all participants, the consultants implemented the competency modeling process. This consisted of the use of paper-and-pencil surveys followed by participant focus groups. During this process participants were asked to offer their responses to four questions:

- What are the specific competencies (skills, behaviors, and knowledge bases) needed for high-level performance as a management team member?
- On a six-point scale, what is each management team member's current level of performance for each of these competencies?
- For competencies where there is a gap between desired and actual performance level, what are the developmental needs?
- How can these developmental needs be met most effectively (for example, training and development or more effective hiring practices)?

The Results. The competency model process yielded consistent results regarding desired and actual competencies. The key skills and abilities were identified as supervisory or leadership skills, training and staff development skills, project planning and management skills, recruitment and selection skills, and communication skills. The key knowledge bases included an understanding of summer engineering program policies and procedures, engineering program participants, campus resources, engineering program curriculum, and various computer applications.

Because the consultants had clearly identified the desired competencies of the management team members, they could then assess the extent to which they currently possessed these competencies and specifically identify performance gaps. Several gaps were identified between actual and desired competencies. They included supervisory and leadership skills, particularly concerning delegation, employee motivation, and staff evaluation; the recruitment and selection of staff; and the training and development of management team employees.

The final step in this process involved the selection of interventions designed to enhance management team skills and abilities in the desired areas; this step involved the systematic use of training and development activities.

Consultants set up a series of developmental workshops on supervisory skills, the interviewing and selection process, and team building. The author also worked with the management team on the creation of a staff development program that could be held on an annual basis. The management team members and department director reported that the process was very successful, and that they would continue to use it in the future.

Concluding Comments

The concepts and practices of performance-based human resource development can play a significant role in student affairs and higher education. Human performance technology (HPT) has the potential to be a useful tool for student affairs departments. When properly applied, HPT can provide for professional staff development in ways that significantly enhance organizational performance. It can benefit student affairs in several ways, most notably in the development of high-quality human performance. A human performance system (HPS) offers several benefits including providing a foundation for the continuous and appropriate development of student affairs professionals, helping student affairs create a greater sense of community within the institution, creating learning environments that benefit students and staff alike, and providing a process for effectively uniting professional development and organizational effectiveness. The challenge for student affairs is to identify the HPT tools and methods that will most effectively address both professional development and institutional performance.

References

American College Personnel Association. *The Student Learning Imperative: Implications for Student Affairs*. Washington, D.C.: American College Personnel Association, 1994.

Bassi, L. J., and Van Buren, M. E. "The 1998 ASTD State of the Industry Report." *Training and Development*, 1998, 52 (1), 21–43.

Birnbaum, R. *How Colleges Work: The Cybernetics of Academic Organizations and Leadership*. San Francisco: Jossey-Bass, 1991.

Brennan, E. J. *Performance Management Workbook*. Englewood Cliffs, N.J.: Prentice Hall, 1989.

Bricker, B. *Info-Line: Basics of Performance Technology*. Alexandria, Va.: American Society for Training and Development, 1992.

Callahan, M. *Info-Line: From Training to Performance Consulting*. Alexandria, Va.: American Society for Training and Development, 1997.

Carnevale, A. P., and Carnevale, E. S. "Growth Patterns in Workplace Training." *Training and Development*, 1994, 48 (5), S22–S28.

Coyne, R. K. "Organization Development: A Broad Net Intervention for Student Affairs." In T. K. Miller and R. B. Winston, Jr. (eds.), *Administration and Leadership in Student Affairs: Actualizing Student Development in Higher Education* (2nd ed.). Muncie, Ind.: Accelerated Development, 1991.

DeCoster, D. A., and Brown, S. S. "Staff Development: Personal and Professional Education." In T. K. Miller and R. B. Winston, Jr. (eds.), *Administration and Leadership in Student Affairs: Actualizing Student Development in Higher Education* (2nd ed.). Muncie, Ind.: Accelerated Development, 1991.

Eitington, J. E. *The Winning Trainer* (2nd ed.). Houston, Tex.: Gulf, 1989.

Fox, D., Kennedy, J., and Vitale, S. "A New Form of Competency Modeling for Lasting Business Results." In W. J. Pfeiffer (ed.), *The 1997 Annual: Consulting*. San Francisco: Pfeiffer/Jossey-Bass, 1997.

Galagan, P. A. "Reinventing the Profession." *Training and Development*, 1994, 48 (12), 20–27.

Gephart, M. A., and Van Buren, M. E. "The Power of High Performance Work Systems." *Training and Development*, 1996, 50 (10), 21–36.

Gill, S. J. "Shifting Gears for High Performance." *Training and Development*, 1995, 49 (5), 24–31.

Gutteridge, T. G., Leibowitz, Z. B., and Shore, J. E. *Organizational Career Development: Benchmarks for Building a World-Class Workforce*. San Francisco: Jossey-Bass, 1993.

Holmes, T. A. *The Human Performance Improvement Worksheet*. Farmington Hills, Mich.: T.A.H. Performance Consultants, 1997 (24907 Woodridge End, 48335).

McLagan, P. A. *Models for HRD Practice: The Models*. Alexandria, Va.: American Society for Training and Development, 1989.

McLagan, P. A. "Competencies: The Next Generation." *Training and Development*, 1997, 51 (5), 40–47.

Mirabile, R. J. "Everything You Wanted to Know About Competency Modeling." *Training and Development*, 1997, 51 (8), 73–77.

Mone, E. M. and Bilger, M. A. "Integrated Human Resource Development: Building Professional Competencies and Communities." In M. London (ed.), *Employees, Careers, and Job Creation: Developing Growth-Oriented Human Resource Strategies and Programs*. San Francisco: Jossey-Bass, 1995.

Preston, F. R. "Creating Effective Staff Development Programs." In M. J. Barr and Associates, *The Handbook of Student Affairs Administration*. San Francisco: Jossey-Bass, 1993.

Rasmussen, T. *The ASTD Trainer's Sourcebook: Diversity, Create Your Own Training Program*. New York: McGraw-Hill, 1996.

Rothwell, W. J. *ASTD Models for Human Performance Improvement: Roles, Competencies and Outputs*. Alexandria, Va.: American Society for Training and Development, 1996.

Stolovitch, H. D., and Keeps, E. J. "What Is Human Performance Technology?" In H. D. Stolovitch and E. J. Keeps (eds.), *Handbook for Human Performance Technology: A Comprehensive Guide for Analyzing and Solving Performance Problems in Organizations*. San Francisco: Jossey-Bass, 1992.

TYRONE A. HOLMES, assistant professor of Counselor Education at Wayne State University, is also president and founder of T.A.H. Performance Consultants, a training and organizational development firm specializing in the enhancement of individual and organizational performance. He has facilitated many HRD programs within both educational and corporate environments, and specializes in performance-based diversity and career development interventions.

Staff development in student affairs is more than isolated events and activities; it should be an integrated staffing function closely tied to supervision.

Staff Supervision and Professional Development: An Integrated Approach

Roger B. Winston, Jr., Don G. Creamer

Staff development in most student affairs circles generally means speakers, teleconferences, workshops, and professional association conferences. In other words, staff development is an event or activity performed outside or beyond daily work duties and activities. Similarly, *supervision* in higher education often means being "called on the carpet" for poor performance or misdeeds. These views of supervision and staff development suggest that competent, well-functioning professionals do not need supervision and that there is little or no logical or practical connection between staff development and supervision.

In this chapter we assert that some of the most effective staff development activities are integrated into the performance of the tasks or responsibilities related to current job assignment, and it is through the supervision process that training and development needs can best be identified and strategies developed to address them. We first present our concept of appropriate supervision, called *synergistic supervision.* Second, we discuss strategies for integrating staff development into normal position responsibilities. Finally, we present a schema to illustrate how supervision and staff development can be integrated.

Synergistic Supervision

The implicit view of supervision in student affairs makes many professionals somewhat uneasy because it seems to suggest inadequacy or subprofessional status for practitioners. Because individual autonomy is highly prized in higher education (Komives, 1992), to suggest that a person needs supervision can be taken to mean that her or his work is unacceptable or that she or he is inadequately prepared to fulfill assigned responsibilities. As a result of these negative attitudes toward supervision, many avoid it or reserve its use to correct grossly inadequate performance or flagrant disregard of propriety.

We propose a different concept of supervision, called synergistic supervision. Supervision should be viewed essentially as a helping process provided by the institution to benefit or support staff rather than as a mechanism for punishment inflicted on practitioners for unsatisfactory performance. Characteristics of synergistic supervision include dual focus; joint effort; two-way communication; focus on competence; goals; systematic, ongoing process; and growth orientation (Winston and Creamer, 1997).

Dual focus. Synergistic supervision focuses both on accomplishing the institution's and unit's goals and on promoting the personal and professional development of staff members. As DeCoster and Brown note, "The ideal framework for professional development is built by interlocking individual and organizational goals" (1991, p. 569). The institution has a legitimate expectation that those it employs are dedicated to promoting accomplishment of its mission; individual professionals also have a legitimate expectation that the institution will show concern for their welfare and provide the support needed for a nourishing work environment and career advancement. An important value of the student affairs field is respect for the worth and dignity of each individual (Young, 1993), whether student or staff employee.

Joint Effort. The synergistic approach to supervision requires a cooperative effort between the supervisor and the supervised. Responsibilities for initiating and maintaining the process fall on the shoulders of both, although supervisors generally should be expected to assume a larger share of the responsibility, because of their more extensive experience in the field and by virtue of their positions in the institutional hierarchy. If the supervisory relationship is to be successful, it is essential that both the supervisor and each staff member invest time and energy in the relationship. Neither party acting alone can make the supervisory process work effectively.

Two-Way Communication. Open and honest communication is necessary to implement the synergistic approach. Implicit in this assertion is the imperative of forming a genuine, respectful, personal relationship between the supervisor and each individual staff member. Lacking this relationship, suggestions for corrections or changes from the supervisor may well be viewed as personal attacks that require defensive reactions. Equally, proposals for change or constructive criticism from a staff member may be viewed with suspicion or as an attempt to undermine the supervisor's authority or reputation in the institution. Absent clear lines of two-way communication, the supervisory process may become meaningless or a disincentive for staff development.

Focus on Competence. Synergistic supervision focuses on four areas of competence: knowledge, work-related skills, personal and professional skills, and attitudes. Each of these areas requires ongoing, although not necessarily equal, attention.

All staff members need to know certain things to carry out their assigned duties. In all areas, staff members need to know about legal constraints to practice, the history of the institution (often highlighting certain issues), its mission, and professional ethical standards. Functional areas require specialized knowledge, such as techniques for designing interventions, computer programming, statistical analysis, student organization advisement, or individual counseling. Staff are expected to possess much of this knowledge when they assume their positions, but changing societal conditions and institutional needs require staff to remain current with contemporary events and sometimes to broaden areas of expertise. (If staff are employed without benefit of a solid student affairs professional education, then supervisors are morally obligated to teach staff members the specific information they need to perform their jobs, basic skills in interpersonal facilitation, and accepted techniques for program development, implementation, and evaluation—in addition to instilling the historical and philosophical foundations of the field.)

Depending on the specific demands of the position, staff members need a multitude of skills such as interpersonal communication, leadership, confrontation, clerical, and research capabilities. Generally, possession of necessary skills is identified in the selection process, but even if staff are proficient when first employed, it remains necessary to stay abreast of changes and new information. Also, staff skills, although once held at a proficient level, may be lost if they are not used regularly.

Another category of professional skills needed by student affairs staff may be classified as "personal and professional." Examples of these skills include writing, time management, stress management, and public speaking. This category of skills blurs the distinctions between personal and professional, but most scholars and seasoned practitioners agree that deficits in these areas result in impaired student affairs practitioners.

Attitude is the final category that should be addressed through the synergistic supervision process and is, perhaps, the most difficult to influence. The attitudes a staff member displays when undertaking a responsibility are often as important or, in some instances, even more important than the actual behavior. Enthusiasm, cynicism, negativism, bitterness, excitement, boredom, cooperation, support, and resistance are examples of attitudes that can have significant effects on staff performance. Because attitudes affect performance, they are legitimate concerns of supervisors. As Mouton and Blake note (1984, pp. 8–9), "Positive attitudes can strongly motivate an individual to apply knowledge and skills to constructive purposes, while negative attitudes can hinder the appropriate use of the knowledge and skills. Aiding individuals to test their attitudes against criteria, and become better aware of how their attitudes influence their thought and behavior" is an important part of the personnel management process.

Modifying attitudes can be a difficult challenge to approach, because evidence of deleterious or obstructive attitudes is difficult to describe objectively.

Some attitudes may be considered *private* and therefore inappropriate for supervisory concern. For instance, attitudes related to politics, religion, and sexual behavior (within the bounds of propriety as defined by professional ethical standards) are generally considered legitimately private and not subject to supervision, especially at public institutions. Unfortunately, the line between private (not subject to direct supervision) and *work-related* (appropriate to address in the supervision process) attitudes is not always clear. Tact and sensitivity are required when dealing with attitudes. Nonetheless, it is essential that staff members understand that their attitudes are a proper subject of supervision *because* of how attitudes affect performance.

There will generally be less resistance to addressing these areas if positive attitudes are regularly commended in addition to problematic attitudes being dealt with. If attitudes are a routine topic during supervisory sessions, when it becomes necessary to deal with troublesome attitudes, staff will be less likely to view the introduction of the topic as impetuous or vindictive. Establishment of a genuinely open, caring relationship between the supervisor and the staff member is the best assurance that the staff member can *hear* the supervisor's concerns and react nondefensively. Staff members who have sufficient evidence that their supervisor wants them to be successful are much more likely to accept constructive criticism and to be willing to take corrective steps.

Although it is difficult, synergistic supervisors must deal directly and openly with staff members' attitudes that affect work performance. They should be vigilant, however, in not allowing the supervisory process to become an attempt to clone staff in their own images; that is, individual differences must be accepted and respected. It is not necessary for supervisors and those supervised to become friends. Such a degree of intimacy is not necessary for effective work relationships and, in fact, may hamper effective supervision.

Goals. Supervision requires a degree of mutually agreed-on structure for the process to be effective. This structure can be built around a series of short and long-term goals that are systematically reviewed and evaluated. By carefully establishing goals, each party in the supervisory process can come to an agreeement about expectations of each other. We further recommend that goals be differentiated as maintenance goals and innovation goals.

To ensure continued quality performance, maintenance goals are important; to encourage creativity and introduce some sense of novelty into position responsibilities, innovation goals should also be set. Most positions in student affairs carry with them some duties or responsibilities that do not challenge experienced practitioners but are important to the welfare of the institution and, therefore, must be done well. At the same time, all positions should have built-in opportunities for innovation; supervisors should encourage staff to take risks and try creative solutions to problems or imaginative new interventions that can positively affect students' personal or educational development.

Systematic, Ongoing Process. In order for the synergistic supervision process to be effective, it must be approached in a methodical manner. Each supervisor and those who are supervised should have regularly scheduled one-on-one sessions for the sole purpose of examining progress in meeting goals, discussing emerging issues or priorities, exchanging views about current activities, identifying potential "hot spots," and revising agreed-on goals. This is also a time for the staff member to solicit advice and guidance from the supervisor about possible ways to attack problems. The timing of these sessions should be based on the experience and competence of the person supervised and the quality of his or her work performance. New staff members—especially at entry level—generally require more frequent sessions than experienced professionals who are performing at an exemplary level. Staff of any seniority who are experiencing problems, of course, require more attention. Synergistic supervision is not used only to correct poor performance—we maintain that every staff member deserves formal supervisory sessions at least four times a year.

Informal, impromptu supervisory sessions should occur as circumstances dictate. When supervisors observe problematic or meritorious performance, they should give immediate feedback (in private) to the staff member. Praise and correction are most effective when given immediately after the activity's occurrence.

Our experience suggests that unless supervisory sessions are planned for and protected from intrusion from daily job demands, they are unlikely to take place. To carefully conceive and execute the supervisory plan vividly demonstrates the importance the activity holds for the organization and the value the institution places on its staff. "For supervisors and staff to communicate effectively and to take shared responsibility, there must be ongoing, systematic, regular attention to the supervision process" (Winston and Creamer, 1997, p. 211).

Growth Orientation. The final characteristic of synergistic supervision is its focus on enhancing the personal and professional growth of staff members. The supervisory process should be deemed a failure if the staff involved do not become better or more proficient in carrying out their responsibilities and have a sense of accomplishment and personal satisfaction in their positions. For the supervisory process to have a growth orientation, it is necessary to help each staff member assess his or her current level of abilities, skills, and knowledge and to explore with the staff member his or her career aspirations, current stage of life development, and expectations of work. The degree to which staff members are invested in higher education and student affairs as a professional endeavor is dependent on the staff member's depth and breadth of experience, educational qualifications, personal and career aspirations, geographical mobility, family situation, and other factors. Supervisors must understand how these forces affect each individual's life and their approach to work when developing goals through the supervisory process.

Career Anchors

One interesting approach to understanding interactive forces in staff lives is through the concept of career anchors developed by Schein (1978; 1990). Career anchors can be thought of as occupational self-concepts composed of three elements: self-perceived talents and abilities based on success in various work settings, self-perceived motives and needs (for example, good income, security, interesting work), and self-perceived attitudes and values (such as the degree of congruence between personal values and institutional values). Through an understanding of staff members' career anchors, supervisors can get a good notion of how they see themselves in relation to their work and what aspects or kinds of work they find especially satisfying. Career anchors provide a window into staff members' primary reasons for working where they do and in what functional area; they can also give some insight into what staff perceive as rewarding in relation to their work (for example, is it money, recognition, autonomy, or internal satisfaction?).

Schein (1990) identifies eight career anchors shared by many people in business, education, and the professions. Following are descriptions of each anchor and an interpretation of how each applies to staff who work in student affairs.

Technical and Functional Competence. Staff with this anchor strive to become experts in a particular area. They tend to be uninterested in general managerial positions such as vice president for student affairs; they seek instead to master their chosen functional area. They may be skilled and talented administrators in their chosen field of specialization; they are, however, uninterested in using those skills in a broader arena. In student affairs, these staff may aspire to be directors of a functional area such as residential life, admissions, financial aid, minority services and programs, or international students. Achievement is defined through further advancement or meeting the challenges within the functional area only.

General Managerial Competence. General managerial competence is what staff with this anchor want to achieve. Acquiring expertise and competence in one or more functional areas is seen as a necessary step in moving toward positions of general administrative responsibility. Staff with this anchor perceive their competence to be in a combination of analytical skills (analyzing and synthesizing complex problems under conditions of incomplete information and uncertainty), interpersonal skills (such as ability to influence and lead others), and emotional competence—they are excited by the challenge of crises, seek high levels of responsibility, and can exercise power without guilt (Schein, 1978). In student affairs, these may be the staff members who aspire to be vice presidents or presidents of institutions.

Security and Stability. Staff with this anchor see their work as a means of ensuring a secure job and a relatively comfortable work environment. The specifics of their assigned tasks may be less important than the sense of refuge the institution offers. They tend to do whatever is asked of them in return for the employment and emotional safety the institution can offer. These staff may become quite devoted to the institution and willing to take a wide range of assignments to *help* the institution. If they have underutilized talents or skills, they may find outside avenues to use them in areas such as charity work, civic involvement, or running a private business. Those who are especially concerned about long-term security issues (permanency of employment, economic health of the institution, retirement plans) and who desire highly predictable work environments tend to hold this anchor.

Creativity. Staff in this category have a great need to build or create something new over which they have control. The opportunity to use the creative process is what makes work attractive to these staff members, who are known for their ability to conceptualize unique and unconventional solutions to problems. In student affairs, they are the staff who are good at creating innovative programs that require ingenuity, charisma, and organizational skills. However, they often lose interest and do not perform well in maintaining their programs once they are established; instead, they are ready to start a new project that presents new challenges to their creativity.

Sense of Service, Dedication to a Cause. Although most professionals in student affairs are attracted to the field because of the humanitarian and philanthropic aspects of educating the nation's youth, other aspects of work (such as achieving technical or managerial competence) may be their preferred means for actualizing their self-perceived talents and skills and meeting their personal needs. Staff with the sense-of-service career anchor are attracted to their work because of their dedication to a cause and because the work allows them the opportunity to further the cause. This anchor can be held by staff in any functional area of student affairs, but it may be encountered most often in areas associated with clearly identified social causes or belief systems such as minority student services, women's centers, religious centers, or gay, lesbian, and bisexual student services. Not all staff in these areas (probably not even a majority), however, hold this career anchor.

Autonomy, or Independence. Staff who hold this career anchor dislike being bound by others' rules, procedures, and time tables. They seek involvement in work that allows them to be their own boss and "to do things their own way, at their own pace, and against their own standards" (Schein, 1990, p. 26). Higher education attracts many people (especially faculty members) who value independence and who chafe at the perceived restrictions imposed in large organizations or bureaucracies. It has been somewhat facetiously noted that tenured faculty members have the freedom associated with self-employment along with the bonus of a regular paycheck for the duration of their work life. In student affairs, staff with an autonomy anchor want their own shops and the freedom to run them as they see fit or to perform services that allow for individual freedom to exercise professional expertise, such as in counseling or medicine.

Pure Challenge. Staff who hold challenge as their career anchor perceive that they can conquer anything or anyone, or they at least want the opportunity to try. Success is operationally defined by them as overcoming impossible odds, "solving unsolvable problems, or winning out over extremely tough opponents" (Schein, 1990, p. 31). Work is generally thought of in competitive terms. In student affairs, staff with challenge as their anchor seek opportunities to put themselves on the line and to demonstrate their superiority. "The areas of work, the kinds of employing organization, the pay system, the type of promotion system, and the forms of recognition are all subordinate to whether or not the job provides constant opportunities for self-tests" (Schein, 1990, p. 31). They are attracted to positions that offer clear ways of "keeping score." Staff with this anchor in student affairs might, for instance, be especially attracted to an admissions position at an institution experiencing enrollment shortfalls or a residence life position in a program that was having difficulty retaining residents. They are energized and motivated by the opportunity to accomplish seemingly impossible tasks.

Lifestyle. Lifestyle as a career anchor seems to be an oxymoron; people with this anchor view their careers as less (or at least no more) important than other things outside work. In other words, they do not have a career anchor but a lifestyle preference. Schein (1990) argues that this anchor is becoming increasingly more prevalent. People who have the lifestyle anchor seek a balanced life that integrates work, leisure, other avocational activities, and family. Lifestyle-anchored staff seek work that allows considerable flexibility in hours and work schedules and benefits that include opportunities for sabbaticals, day care, and parental leaves, for example. Student affairs staff members with this anchor may have lifestyle interests other than those associated with family that they desire to integrate with work, such as pursuit of leisure activities that may require considerable time on occasions that conflict with the academic calendar. Staff with this anchor may not be attracted to any particular functional area; they often are looking for the best fit between their work interests and other outside interests. Work is seen primarily as a means to achieve or afford a particular lifestyle.

Staff Development

Many writers on this topic (Burke and Randall, 1994; DeCoster and Brown, 1991; Winston and Creamer, 1997; Winston, Hebert, and McGonigle, 1985; Woodard and Komives, 1990) argue that for maximum effectiveness, staff development activities should be integrated with the staff supervision and performance appraisal processes. Viewed from this perspective, staff development is a complex, multidimensional process. As with the supervision process, staff development has a dual focus: enhancement of individual professional and personal knowledge and skills and of organizational functioning and accomplishment of the institution's mission. Staff development must be approached with an understanding of each individual staff member's level of personal development, career anchor, educational background, breadth and depth of professional experience, and level of professional development and the level of maturity, stability, and structure of the institution and its organizational culture.

Determining Staff Development Needs. To adopt the synergistic approach to supervision advocated here, some of the first things that must be done to form an appropriate context for staff development are to establish an open, trusting relationship between staff member and supervisor; determine each staff member's career anchor; identify professional aspirations of staff; and identify necessary knowledge and skills required of staff to advance professionally. Concurrently, the unit's problems and goals and the institutional problems and mission must be identified and addressed in making staff development plans.

Ideally, through a process that includes all members of the unit, problems and aspirations should be identified and strategies for addressing them formulated. Because of this process, specific unit or department goals should be formulated and strategies should be designed to accomplish them. In developing the strategies for accomplishing the goals, assignments and responsibilities for individual staff members will naturally need to be made part of individuals' work assignments. Individually and privately, the supervisor and each staff member should analyze what skills and knowledge are needed to successfully accomplish the assignments and determine the extent to which the staff member currently possesses them. When new knowledge or skills are needed, skill acquisition should become one of the goals for the staff member that are developed through the supervision process.

Developing Interpersonal Relationships. For staff development and supervision to be integrated, there must first be an open, trusting relationship between the staff member and the supervisor. Lacking such a relationship, staff members may be reluctant to admit knowledge or skill deficiencies, because they legitimately fear that such information may be used against them. Similarly, the supervisor's observations about shortcomings may be viewed as a personal attack if a trusting relationship has not first been established. It is essential that staff members believe that their supervisor has their best interests at heart and truly wants them to be successful.

Understanding Staff Members' Life and Career Goals. In addition to identifying organizational needs, individual interests and aspirations must be considered. As mentioned earlier, an exploration of a staff member's career anchor and long- and intermediate-term personal and professional goals is necessary. Through an understanding of career anchors, supervisors can capture insight into how each staff member views his or her work and what (in addition to increased pay) each considers motivation or reward for good performance. It also is important to understand where each staff member wants to go. Are there personal or family issues that affect professional plans? How important is professional advancement to the staff member? Is the staff member geographically limited?

Important to understanding staff members is an awareness of their current developmental status. Just as we need to understand students' psychosocial and intellectual development to facilitate their learning and development, we also need to understand the content and process of development experienced by staff members. (See Winston and Creamer (1997) for a brief summary of psychosocial development issues faced by student affairs professionals.) Carpenter (1991) presents a model of professional development that may help both staff members and supervisors determine current developmental status and identify knowledge, skills, and experiences that may be needed to advance profession-ally. His model specifies four stages of professional development: formative (preparing to enter and initial entry to the field), application (perfecting skills and finding a niche in the field), additive (making value-added contributions to the field and the employing institution), and generative (assuming upper-level leadership, sharing wealth of experience with others, nurturing the pro-fession).

Meeting Individual and Organizational Needs. Using the schema pre-sented in Figure 3.1, staff members and supervisors can classify established goals for staff development and determine whether there is an appropriate bal-ance between meeting the needs of the institution and those of the individual. Should there be an imbalance, new or replacement goals may need to be for-mulated.

Integration of Individual and Organizational Needs

DeCoster and Brown (1991) suggest that staff development activities can be conceptualized in three categories: knowledge, skills, and personal qualities. If we take DeCoster and Brown's classification together with common meth-ods or avenues available for addressing acquisition of each staff development outcome, a taxonomy of alternative means for staff development of knowl-edge, skills, or personal qualities can be produced. Avenues or methods can be classified according to their availability on or off campus. Thus, the feasi-

Figure 3.1. Taxonomy of Staff Development Goals

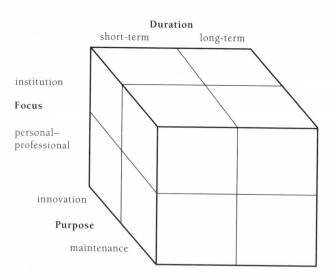

bility of achieving each goal is made more evident. Table 3.1 summarizes this taxonomy.

Additional comment may be helpful to fully understand several staff development avenues, namely, self-directed study, job redesign, shadowing, conducting a research study, service on interdepartmental committee or task force, and special projects.

Facilitating Self-Directed Study. The primary responsibility for improving professional knowledge and skills rests with the individual staff member. Consequently, it is reasonable to expect staff members to take steps to fill gaps in knowledge or skill on their own initiative. If, however, staff need to learn a substantial amount of new material, supervisors should offer support in shifting job responsibilities to allow time for self-study.

Redesigning Jobs. This is often the most effective and cost-efficient means of staff development. As staff members identify or envision their next professional position and where they plan to be in five to ten years, they may identify skills and experiences that their current position offers little or no opportunity to acquire. It is often possible for position descriptions to be refined or altered to give a staff member the kinds of experience he or she needs to meet their goals. One of the most popular approaches for entry-level staff is to split position responsibilities between residential life and another area

Table 3.1. Staff Development Avenues for Acquiring Knowledge, Skills, and Personal Qualities

Avenues	Knowledge	Skills	Personal Qualites
On campus			
Self-directed study	*	+	
Read professional literature	*		*
Take course[1]	*	*	*
Job redesign	*	*	*
Shadowing	*	*	*
Conduct research study	*	*	
Involvement in interdepartmental committee/task force	*	*	*
Undertake special project	*	+	*
Volunteer for special assignment	*	*	*
Off campus			
Professional association conference	*		*
Involvement in professional association	*	*	*
Attend workshop	*	*	

Note: Asterisk indicates avenue is ideal for meeting needs; plus sign indicates avenue may assist in meeting needs but is not ideal; no symbol means avenue is not well suited for meeting needs.

[1]Most likely to be available only on large campuses with extensive graduate programs.

of student affairs, such as student activities, admissions, or international students. This is most common on smaller campuses, where multiple areas of responsibility are customary, but the same can be accomplished on large campuses; it simply requires greater effort and more coordination.

Another approach that has proven successful, especially among several staff members of equal rank, is to reassess position requirements and make new assignments appropriate to the findings of the assessment and to staff development needs. When a position becomes vacant, the interests and needs of the remaining staff are considered before advertising the position's duties. It may be possible to redistribute responsibilities so that the duties for the new position are not the same as they were for the previous holder. In fact, distribution of responsibilities can be achieved even without a position vacancy if the affected staff are cooperative. This latter opportunity suggests that systematic and ongoing position analysis within a student affairs unit or division is sound practice and that its consequences may yield powerful opportunities for staff development without incurring great costs.

Shadowing. On many campuses, shadowing—having a staff member accompany and observe another staff member performing his or her duties—has been a popular approach in new-staff orientation. This can be an effective technique to help a staff member, especially in a first job, gain a better understanding about other areas of student affairs and how they relate to the staff member's area of responsibility. It can also be an effective tool to assist young staff as they do more in-depth career exploration and consider pursuing other jobs in the field.

Conducting a Research Study. Unfortunately, many people enter student affairs lacking extensive research experience, and many express apprehension about the process, especially as they contemplate further graduate study. An effective means of integrating staff development and institutional needs is to form a research team, headed by an experienced researcher, and assign to the team the responsibility of investigating an issue or problem important to the institution. Staff members can gain valuable experience and build their self-confidence in this area, especially if the person heading the team structures it to be a learning experience.

Involvement in Interdepartmental Committees or Task Forces. An excellent learning opportunity is available to staff through involvement in institutional or interdepartmental student affairs committees and task forces. It is important, however, for such assignments to be made in light of the staff member's developmental needs rather than just on the basis of willingness to contribute or interests. Supervisors need a clear understanding about which of these groups are likely to produce valuable learning opportunities and which are extensions of a mindless bureaucracy that simply require the physical presence of some staff member.

Special Projects. Special projects may be fortuitously or intentionally provided. Fortuitous opportunities may arise from unanticipated demands on a unit, such as the need to develop new mechanisms for using advanced educational technologies. On many campuses, summer means reduced workloads and a time when projects can be crafted with an eye toward creating opportunities for staff development. Such opportunities should be seized by designing special projects for staff members that will address an institutional need while also exposing staff members to new responsibilities or to a student clientele to which they have had little or no exposure.

Concluding Comments

Staff development in student affairs is an integrated staffing function closely tied to synergistic forms of supervision. Synergistic supervision strives to achieve both institutional and individual goals and results from intentionally derived plans crafted by each staff member in a context of ongoing supervision. Synergism in supervision and the use of career anchors as a window through which staff developmental orientation can be viewed in planning for staff development were clarified in the chapter.

Goals for staff development should be set in an appropriate institutional context, and this process was highlighted by suggesting a taxonomy of staff development goals that help ensure a balance of goals. Further assistance in crafting staff development plans was offered in the form of a scheme to analyze available methods or avenues for pursuing jointly determined goals. Finally, several attractive staff development opportunities were briefly described.

References

Burke, T. H., and Randall, K. P. "Developing an Organizational Commitment to Employee Success: The Student Affairs Staff Development Model." *College Student Affairs Journal,* 1994, 13 (1), 73–81.

Carpenter, D. S. "Student Affairs Profession: A Developmental Perspective." In T. K. Miller, R.B. Winston, Jr., and others, *Administration and Leadership in Student Affairs: Actualizing Student Development in Higher Education* (2nd ed.). Muncie, Ind.: Accelerated Development, 1991.

DeCoster, D. A., and Brown, S. S. "Staff Development: Personal and Professional Education." In T. K. Miller, R.B. Winston, Jr., and others, *Administration and Leadership in Student Affairs: Actualizing Student Development in Higher Education* (2nd ed.). Muncie, Ind.: Accelerated Development, 1991.

Komives, S. R. "The Middles: Observations on Professional Competence and Autonomy." *NASPA Journal,* 1992, 29, 83–90.

Mouton, J. S., and Blake, R. R. *Synergogy: A New Strategy for Education, Training, and Development.* San Francisco: Jossey-Bass, 1984.

Schein, E. H. *Career Dynamics: Matching Individual and Organizational Needs.* Reading, Mass.: Addison-Wesley, 1978.

Schein, E. H. *Career Anchors: Discovering Your Real Values.* San Francisco: Pfeiffer, 1990.

Winston, R. B., Jr., and Creamer, D. G. *Improving Staffing Practices in Student Affairs.* San Francisco: Jossey-Bass, 1997.

Winston, R. B., Jr., Hebert, D. A., and McGonigle, R. B. "Professional Staff Development as Management Tool." *College Student Affairs Journal,* 1985, 6 (2), 12–25.

Woodward, D. B., Jr., and Komives, S. R. "Ensuring Staff Competence." In M. J. Barr, M. L. Upcraft, and Associates, *New Futures for Student Affairs: Building a Vision for Professional Leadership and Practice.* San Francisco: Jossey-Bass, 1990.

Young, R. B. "The Essential Values of the Profession." In R. B. Young (ed.), *Identifying and Implementing the Essential Values of the Profession.* New Directions for Student Services, no. 61. San Francisco: Jossey-Bass, 1993.

ROGER B. WINSTON, JR. is professor of college student affairs administration at the University of Georgia.

DON G. CREAMER is professor of education and coordinator of college student affairs and higher education programs at Virginia Polytechnic and State University.

New professionals in student affairs must be nurtured to become essential contributors to the profession.

Creating a Culture of Development for the New Professional

Patricia J. Harned, Michael C. Murphy

The Stage

The recruitment, retention, development, and advancement of entry-level professionals are critical to any organization. For those embarking on a path toward meaningful student affairs work, the relationship with one's first immediate supervisor can be critical in creating a lasting commitment to the field. Institutional climate, the availability in an institution of professional development opportunities, resources, and a shared understanding of institutional philosophy are also essential to the satisfaction and nurturance of new professionals (Murphy, Harned, Lipscomb, and O'Brien, 1991).

The first steps in a new professional's experience are critical to his or her long-term success. No relationship holds greater natural potential to influence self-image, career satisfaction, and professional development than the relationship with a supervisor. Ideally, a supervisor will possess a keen sensitivity to the needs and concerns of staff members and have an unwavering dedication to their development. Similarly new professionals in student affairs may be focused on their own growth and personal health and may be partnered with and developed by many individuals in their work. Their success in contributing to the institution's educational process is dependent on the relationships among these interests.

A common touchstone in this chapter is quantitative and qualitative data from a national study of new professionals and supervisors of new professionals (Murphy, Harned, Lipscomb, and O'Brien, 1991). Our understanding of the importance of personal and professional development for the new professional has been enhanced by our own academic and professional experiences. It is our intent in this chapter to stimulate thoughtful discussion, not to suggest a prescriptive remedy.

Essential Elements

Among the many elements involved in the development of the new professional, four are identified as critical and essential: the new professional, the supervisor, the institutional leadership, and the student affairs leadership. Other members of the institutional community, colleagues, faculty, administrators, mentors, government officials, and family members are critical to the educational process. The focus here is primarily on these four critical factors, the interrelationships among them, and the vision they share.

To understand the dynamic relationships among the four factors, it is important to discern how their commonality of focus creates an environment in which the new professional's development is cultivated. The ability to diminish the areas where only one or two of the factors intersect, and to accentuate the areas where all four share common purpose, helps the new professional and the institution overall. The more each factor works in concert with the others, the larger the field of commonality and potential for growth.

The Institution. Several common themes emerge across 3,000 institutions of higher education despite divergent institutional dynamics. Human nature and the economics of higher education create a climate of institutional tension that influences professional development as it does other institutional dynamics. For the new professional, seeing through the inspirational rhetoric of mission statements and goals to find and understand the nature of institutional commitment to broad-based student development is not easy. As a result, those entering our field often find themselves in work environments that are unstable, confusing, and conflicting (Evans, 1988).

Genuine institutional commitment is not the only variable in the development of an ideal campus climate; resources are perhaps the most important catalyst or inhibitor. The necessary and appropriate demands for salary, operating and capital expenditures for research, and core academic initiatives are significant limiting factors in many institutions. The commitment is not to new professionals but reflects on the institutional infrastructure that creates the developmental climate for all students and staff.

The Profession. Few professions can equal student affairs' direct commitment to young professionals. Much attention at national conferences and in organizational literature is given to the foundation that young professionals provide for our organizational hierarchies. Student affairs preparation programs, though criticized from time to time (as are preparatory programs in other professions), show keen sensitivity to the welfare of new professionals. There is no shortage of core ideology in our literature and classrooms. Our young professionals pursue their graduate study with great vigor and enthusiasm. Research suggests that "knowledge gained through practice, internships, and assistantships," as well as "supervisory or mentor relationships that foster professional development and understanding" appear to equip new staff members for their first professional positions so "they are not as easily disillusioned" as we might expect (Richmond and Sherman 1991, p. 16). Unfortunately the profession is less successful in the direct and ongoing support of young professionals at work. While many lament the second-class standing of student affairs in higher education, there often has not been an explicit effort to bolster institutional commitment to cultivate better compensation and rewards for our new professionals.

The Supervisor. There may be few organizations as deprived of traditional managerial and supervisory training and development protocols as colleges and universities. In educational organizations, the intellectual and artistic community, narrowly defined, is one which thrives on a level of delegation of authority and independence of action that is not readily translatable to the other aspects of the institution. Business operations, including development, university relations, and core auxiliaries, often seem anomalous with their traditional organizational constructs and their real-world applications of management theory. Still, they often suffer from resource constraints that leave them operating with high turnover and with less supervisory and managerial support than might be the case in a parallel for-profit organization.

Supervisors in a student affairs setting have limited role models in the institution. They often have little formal managerial training or expertise. They have a strong developmental orientation, which often translates well into a climate of nurturance and support, but the lack of strategic planning and resource orchestration is often an Achilles heel. After two to four years in an entry-level position, most practitioners seek more responsible positions in supervisory roles (Wood, Winston, and Polkosnik, 1985). A common dynamic is that a star professional is promoted into a managerial position with little or no true preparation, where the fallback to avoid failure is not better supervision but harder work. This can create an unhealthy situation that may result in resentment and disenchantment by both overwrought supervisors and neglected staff.

The New Professional. It is in this influential context of the institution, the profession, and the supervisor that the new professional's first job experience is framed. Although it may be true that most new student affairs staff fall into the profession through an engaging undergraduate experience, rather than through some longstanding professional vision, the dedication and passion of our new professionals is our greatest asset. The student affairs field is energized by fresh new faces at national conferences every year. The fire burns brightly much to the credit of institutional paraprofessional communities and graduate preparation programs.

Unfortunately, the fire is often dimmed early. New professionals, even those who have positive relationships with their supervisors, are often displeased with the compensation, advancement opportunities, and operational resources for student services (Baumgartner, 1991). In our study, dissatisfaction was found with training, formal education opportunities, office accommodations, and provision of clerical and support services. These pragmatic concerns overshadowed the strong positive responses to relationships with students, staff, and peers and the softer but still positive ratings of organizational philosophy, autonomy, opportunity to pursue varied interests, and institutional reputation (Murphy, Harned, Lipscomb, and O'Brien, 1991).

A critical question that supervisors, institutional leaders, and leaders in student affairs must ask and answer is, Can these concerns be allowed to determine whether young experienced student affairs professionals leave the profession for other employment opportunities? This scenario does not serve the student affairs profession well. Do we create an infrastructure that provides opportunities for solid experience, responsibility and rewards so the long-term viability of the profession can be a reality for many rather than few? This is a very difficult question and the answer may be unsettling.

The Relationships

In the institutional framework, the potential to create a climate for new professional growth and development is exciting. As with any system, strengths must be identified and enhanced. A division of student affairs must act in an integrated fashion to build on the following six critical relationships among the four players in the structure of the institution.

Profession–Institution Relationship. Most student affairs professionals are familiar with collegial and professional association discussions on the question, Is this a profession? Often, coming through this discourse is a message that we are unsure of how faculty value our work. Reports of alienation between the academic and nonacademic initiatives or chasms between student affairs and upper-level administration permeate professional literature and much of the discussion at our national conferences. Ironically, it seems that no one holds student affairs in lower esteem than we do. Student affairs staff members project a sentiment of inherent disutility rarely echoed by faculty or senior administrators. As student affairs professionals, we have difficulty in directly measuring the impact of our work. The loftiest ambitions are scarcely measurable, and so the sense of new professionals that others do not understand or value their work is reinforced, inadvertently or otherwise, in the profession itself.

Vision. The shared vision between the profession and institutions is driven by a mandate from student affairs leaders, born of an alliance with corporate and government leaders committed to developing the potential of students we accept and the final product we produce, the graduate. The message of our professional roles must be clear, concise, and unambiguous, though the delivery in the institutional setting will depend on circumstance. Much has been done by the profession to articulate this vision, but less has been done to engender a commitment to that vision by constituencies outside the institution, so our vision has met with widely disparate levels of success.

A strong vision must embrace the core issues of creating and disseminating knowledge. Ironically, the profession has not done enough to enhance the intellectual and artistic missions of higher education institutions. Although what we do is an essential foundation for all human endeavor, the bridge into the academic and artistic soul of the institution is often untraversed by both new professionals and senior student affairs staff. The worst fears often become a self-fulfilling prophecy. "The most basic focus of our professional activity ought to foster and support to the best of our abilities the holistic development of the student *and* the development of the institution" (Williams, 1988, pp. 404–405).

Barriers. Student affairs, as a profession, faces several barriers: resource constraints, many demands, and separation from the primary institutional mission of creation and dissemination of knowledge. The result is a limited impact on institutional decision making that can potentially curtail existing opportunities for professional development, research, and contribution by practitioners. These barriers limit our profession. They also confound younger staff members as they attempt to become successful.

Enablers. To strengthen the relationship between institutions and the profession, student affairs professionals must work with everyone from corporate recruiters to politicians; the results better prepare the students we influence. Skills needed to be successful graduates include: character, integrity, sensitivity, intercultural fluency, confidence, and leadership. Often these skills have been developed through student cocurricular experiences. The product is good. The demand is ubiquitous. These skills and knowledge must be enhanced, and student affairs professionals can be the catalyst for that transformation.

Strategies. Potential strategies on which to build the profession–institution relationship include the following:

- Institutional commitment to involvement in the field beyond periodic presentations at national conferences (for example, the encouragement of mid- and upper-level managers in universities to assume leadership positions in the field).
- Professional organization efforts to bring our well-crafted and thoughtful mission(s) more clearly into focus by our corollary professional academic, accrediting, administrative, corporate, and governmental agencies and organizations.
- A commitment by professional organization leaders and the general membership to focus on initiatives that build awareness of and commitment to the value of student affairs' influence on students.

Although the many benefits of a closer association between institutions and the profession are clear, the most salient benefits are the potential for increased resource allocation, more professional validation, enhanced impact and cross-functional facility, and in-field mobility for new professionals.

Profession–New Professional Relationship. Professional associations may have the greatest relevance to the new professional. Professional associations provide a vehicle for new professionals to job search, meet other professionals, and reunite with graduate school classmates. Professional associations offer new professionals the opportunity to establish a network with colleagues from other institutions. It is encouraging that many presentations at national conferences are conducted (or co-conducted) by and designed for new professionals in the field.

Clearly these opportunities provide an intellectual and collegial haven for new professionals. In a similar way, preparation programs provide the venue for new professionals to gain information about professional organizations, while providing a solid foundation of our ideology and history.

Vision. Although it has been previously suggested that our profession could better serve new professionals through a tighter profession–institution relationship, the immediate relationship seems well met, and is a well-established source of satisfaction for new professionals (Murphy, Harned, Lipscomb, and O'Brien, 1991). The central question under consideration is whether the profession may pursue better mechanisms to ensure that new professionals are well prepared for the realities of the profession.

Barriers. The primary barriers to these suggestions are capacity for time and institutional commitment for new professionals to maintain that connection. Our survey (Murphy, Harned, Lipscomb, and O'Brien, 1991) suggests that new professionals entering the field are encouraged as graduate students to become actively involved in leadership roles, to read journals in the field, and to submit work for publication. But many new professionals say that this encouragement dissipates quickly as less than half maintain these activities into their professional years (Murphy, Harned, Lipscomb, and O'Brien, 1991; Richmond and Sherman, 1991).

Enablers. Enabling the connection between the new professional and the student affairs profession at large are new professional involvements, association with other professionals with similar interests, and services such as placement activities that draw new professionals to annual conferences.

Strategies. Potential strategies to enhance these relationships include greater attention to pairing new professionals with upper-level administrators and faculty in the field, encouragement of continued new professional involvement in professional activities at conferences, suggestions as to how new professionals can benefit the profession beyond contributions to professional organizations, and institutional allocation of staff time and resources for professional development initiatives.

Profession–Supervisor Relationship. Those who most closely observe the trying circumstances of the new professional are often supervisors of new professionals. Through extraordinary talent and often sheer tenacity, these supervisors inherit a critical role in our profession: the nurturance and support of those entering the field. As noted, it is a role for which they are often eager and empathic, but ill prepared. As the discussion continues, we next focus on the connection between the profession and supervisors.

Vision. Student affairs educators have argued that the profession is well connected philosophically and pragmatically to and with new professionals. Our vision is for the profession to provide continuing education for supervisors of new professionals and to create a forum for interaction with other supervisors, advice, and new strategies for supervision. This process should include communication of a professional philosophy by which personal practices can be gauged against a larger professional perspective of new staff development. It may also include increased support for institutional investment in supervision training and time. The development of "specific skills and exposure to new approaches and resource uses" for mid-level staff "have been identified as the two most valuable benefits from participation in continuing education programs" (Miller, 1975, p. 263).

Barriers. This integral connection between supervisors of new professionals and the profession itself faces few barriers. The most significant one is time, but enhanced supervision may create more time. Perhaps the most pressing issue is the delayed impact of an investment in supervisory training and attention that requires patience to realize the reward. Both new professionals and supervisors value this relationship; it is an important delivery vehicle founded on mutual respect.

Enablers. Our role is that of educator and counselor. The transfer of these skills to effective supervision is clear. Though clear, it is not automatic, so we must capture the notion of concern for the welfare of staff, and decrease the cost of separation and turnover by using good training to protect our investment.

Strategies. Strategies to build the supervisor–profession connection include managerial training programs targeted to student affairs professionals, explicit graduate training for eventual engagement of this role, regular forums at national conferences to share ideas and experience among the supervisors of new professionals, and better evaluation and training tools for supervisors for use with new professionals.

Institution–Supervisor Relationship. Supervisors of new professionals are often mid-level managers in the administration. As a result, many of their concerns for professional development and direction are echoed by new professionals. To the new professional, supervisors are the embodiment of the institution as they train and make decisions regarding the direction and activities of the new professional. "New professionals in particular sometimes must walk a thin line between the needs of students and professional commitments and the requirements of the institution" (Kinser, 1993, p. 8). In many ways, supervisors are more responsible for the relationship between the new professional and the institution. For this reason alone, the supervisor–institution relationship is critical to the development of the new professional.

Vision. Our vision is for a supervisor supported by and in turn supportive of the institutional mission. The recognition of supervision, especially the supervision of new professionals and support staff, should be a key element of personal and institutional success.

Barriers. This vision can be limited by a supervisor's lack of knowledge of or commitment to the institutional mission; lack of opportunity for advancement that may preclude deep and long lasting commitment to the institution, staff, and its students; lack of an institutional vision (community and its activities); and lack of a vision for mid-level manager training and development and the resulting commitment of resources.

Enablers. Enablers to this relationship include the proven talent of most supervisors of new professionals as they have risen beyond the crowded entry level of the profession, the supervisor's strong commitment to the field and genuine desire for institutional affinity, and the energizing nature of the task of nurturing young professionals for the supervisor.

Strategies. Specific strategies to build the new supervisor–institution connection include more deliberate engagement in the development of supervisors by senior student affairs administrators in issues of cross-institutional relevance, a determined effort by senior student affairs administrators to create opportunities for supervisors to be involved with faculty and other junior administrators on cross-functional teams and task forces, and the allocation of time so that supervisors of new professionals can become familiar with academic and administrative units in the institution.

Institution–New Professional Relationship. Institutional *fit* is very important to new professionals when selecting a place of employment in their first professional role. Institutional values, direction, and character are also critical to new professionals as they assume positions. New professionals are quite concerned about the nature and reputation of their institutions (Murphy, Harned, Lipscomb, and O'Brien, 1991). The strongest influence in this relationship is the immediate supervisor, which we address in detail now.

Vision. Our vision for the new professional is to become engaged in contributing to, supporting, and passing on institutional values to members of the campus community. Whatever their area of specialization, new professionals must embody the fullest set of institutional values and foci. The nature of influence on students is commonly going to be a generalist influence born of a relationship of trust emerging from some residential, service, or employment base. This is a profound dynamic. It might be said that although an institutional vantage point is always desired, there are some industries where it is not critical to have that vantage point to perform a front-line function. Although this trend is not true in student affairs work, we must still dedicate considerable energy toward forging this relationship—the bond between the new professional and the institution—right from the start.

Barriers. Quite pragmatically, most new professionals begin their employment in July and are fully immersed in hard work by August. There is little time to develop a broader perspective, and it is not easy to gain access to key institutional players during that period. Universities are complicated beasts, often embodying a labyrinth of organizational structures and curious vestiges of organizational design. Even the most experienced veteran administrator can be taxed to maintain cross-institutional contact, service, and management. Further, there is little historic validation for new professionals' engagement in or exposure to the research and curricular life of the institution, leaving them outside what could be considered the most fundamental teacher–student dynamic available. This entry period for a new professional becomes "a time for developing a high tolerance for ambiguity" (Kirby, 1984, p. 28), and, as previously stated, "our primary attitude must be one of adaptability and flexibility" (Moore, 1984, p. 69).

Enablers. The new professional–institutional connection includes new professionals' eagerness and loyalty to the institution of their employment, supervisor familiarity with key individuals on campus, and the need for fresh perspectives and hard work at all institutional levels, creating potential entrees for new professionals to be involved in initiatives throughout the campus.

Strategies. Potential strategies include the following:

- Encouragement and opportunities (operational, educational, or social) for the new professional to interact with faculty, upper-level administration, and other staff to gain a sense of institutional activities.
- Encouragement for new professionals to take a class, sit in on a class, and visit labs and studios to gain a sense of student perspective.
- Reinforcement of the idea that programs should be based on known campus needs and geared toward identified institutional interest.
- Support for experienced faculty and staff to develop a hosting or mentoring relationship with new professionals in their institution.

Supervisor–New Professional Relationship. As is already evident, no relationship has the potential for more sustained impact than that of the new professional and the immediate supervisor. A supervisor has the potential to become a mentor for staff entering our field. "With the right supervisor, all kinds of opportunities to explore the field and to better understand the profession become available" (Birch, 1984, p. 46). Many new professionals assume their first professional positions expecting to be apprenticed to their supervisors, and may eagerly await their directives for office operation, career advice, and involvement opportunities in the field. Given the limits of tangible validation and reward in our field, it is often the supervisor to whom the new professional looks for reinforcement and reassurance.

Vision. Our vision for the new professional and supervisor is to become engaged in a challenging, developmental relationship, preparing the new professional for both short- and long-term professional success. This may even extend to long-term personal success, as a good supervisor can help new professionals guard against being overwhelmed by many daunting challenges.

Barriers. It is common to presume that good people set loose on a task will excel, and there is evidence to support the claim, but a sustained and nurturing relationship is essential for long-term success. It can be difficult, for supervisors and new professionals alike, to take the time to invest in the kind of relationship that yields long-term foundational results when immediate needs and service demands are so pressing. The irony of the demand is that a solid supervisor–new professional relationship can be a source of efficiency and impact, but it is a largely unmeasured variable. Institutions and professional leaders must recognize and act on this opportunity. Solid training programs must be created lest supervisors have difficulty inspiring and leading new professionals.

Enablers. The connection between the new professional and his or her supervisor cannot be easily quantified or qualified. The greatest resource is the generally unselfish nature of people in student affairs. We tend to build relationships, seek consensus, and have a genuine concern for others. Student affairs operations seek an environment guided by the principles that frame our service to students. Supervisor support, time dedicated to new professionals, nurturing attitudes, and patience are endemic to the new supervisor and new professional relationship (Murphy, Harned, Lipscomb, and O'Brien, 1991). Student affairs is a field with many opportunities but many difficulties, so it is often the primary supervisor who must sort out these competing perspectives so the new professional can succeed.

Strategies. Critical strategies for enhancing the supervisor–new professional relationship include clear expectations for frequent interaction and feedback; development of a personal goal statement to use as the basis for meeting the new professional's needs; periodic evaluations of and by both the new professional and the supervisor; explicit exploration of areas for growth and attention to strategies to meet those objectives; and resources to accommodate common needs such as compensation, professional development support, staffing, and advancement (Murphy, Harned, Lipscomb, and O'Brien, 1991).

Concluding Comments

New professionals and their supervisors are critical players in the profession and the institution, and those in each group need special support and guidance. Each has an obligation to create opportunities for growth and development for one another, for their host institutions, and for our profession.

The development of the new professional is serious work. It is at the very core of what we do. Simple in some ways, this level of professional development is by no means automatic. As a profession, we must explore the supports currently in place to build esteem and competence among new professionals as well as determine those that are missing. Our institutional leadership must commit to use the resources necessary to create a positive climate for both new professionals and their supervisors.

Supervisors of new professionals must take the task seriously. They must commit the time and energy to tailor the experiences of new professionals for maximum impact. New professionals must understand that there is hard work ahead. There is potential for many rewards so an investment in their own growth and development will pay many dividends in the future.

These important relationships, though complex, must bow to the universal foundations of human connectedness. Shared vision, mutual respect, commitment to the welfare of others, personal responsibility, selflessness, risk taking, hard work, positive environment, integrity, efficiency and open communications are ingredients for success in no way unique to our field of endeavor. What is unique in this vision is that lifelong personal success of all people in our college and university communities can be realized. Those entering our field have a depth of character and commitment to this vision that is our most precious asset.

References

Baumgartner, D. *The Student Affairs Professional: A Study of the Private Colleges in Iowa.* East Lansing, Mich.: National Center for Research on Teacher Learning, May 1991. (ED 350 939)

Birch, J. W. "Thoughts on Career Advancement." In A. F. Kirby and D. Woodard (eds.), *Career Perspectives in Student Affairs.* NASPA Monograph Series, vol. I. U.S.A.: The National ASDA, 1984.

Evans, N. "Attrition of Student Affairs Professionals: A Review of the Literature." *Journal of College Student Development,* 1988, 29, 19–24.

Kinser, K. *New Professionals in Student Affairs: What They Didn't Teach You in Graduate School.* East Lansing, Mich.: National Center for Research on Teacher Learning, 1993. (ED 378 491)

Kirby, A. F. "The New Professional." In A. F. Kirby and D. Woodard (eds.), *Career Perspectives in Student Affairs.* NASPA Monograph Series, vol. I. U.S.A.: The National ASDA, 1984.

Miller, T. K. "Staff Development in Student Affairs Programs." *Journal of College Student Personnel,* 1975, 16 (4), 258–264.

Moore, L. V. "Summary Thoughts and a Look to the Future." In A. F. Kirby and D. Woodard, (eds.), *Career Perspectives in Student Affairs.* NASPA Monograph Series, vol. I. U.S.A.: The National ASDA, Inc., 1984.

Murphy, M. C., Harned, P. J., Lipscomb, L. J., and O'Brien, D. A. "Supervising the New Professional: Developing the Leaders of the Future." Paper presented at the annual convention of the American College Personnel Association, Atlanta, Ga., 1991.

Richmond, J. and Sherman, K. J. "Student-Development Preparation and Placement: A Longitudinal Study of Graduate Students and New Professionals' Experiences." *Journal of College Student Development,* 1991, 32 (1), 8–16.

Williams, T. E. "Toward a Professional Paradigm: In Search of a Philosophy." *Journal of College Student Development,* 1988, 29 (5), 403–405.

Wood, L., Winston, R. B., Jr., and Polkosnik, M. C. "Career Orientations and Professional Development of Young Student Affairs Professionals." *Journal of College Student Personnel,* 1985, 26 (6), 532–539.

PATRICIA J. HARNED began her professional career as an assistant to the dean of student affairs at Carnegie Mellon University, working with Michael C. Murphy. Currently she is a teaching fellow and graduate researcher at the University of Pittsburgh.

MICHAEL C. MURPHY is the dean of student affairs at Carnegie Mellon University. He began his career as a new professional at Carnegie Mellon, and has supervised numerous new professionals and supervisors of new professionals in a variety of student service areas during his sixteen-year tenure.

The impact of mentoring on those entering and advancing in the field of student affairs, the protégés; those providing professional development support, the mentors; and the organizations that they serve is complex and developmentally important.

Influence and Impact: Professional Development in Student Affairs

Diane L. Cooper, Theodore K. Miller

Most student affairs practitioners would agree that formal academic professional education provides an excellent, perhaps essential, foundation on which to build a professional career. Nevertheless, a two-year master's degree, even with the addition of three or more years of doctoral study, cannot be expected to provide complete and total professional development in itself. Although the fundamental knowledge, philosophy, theory, models, applications, and skills that undergird formal professional education are clearly influential, both the personal, affective development and the cognitive, conceptual development so essential to professional practice are similarly influenced tremendously by those with whom the developing student affairs practitioner works and otherwise associates. It is this latter dimension of professional development that this chapter explores.

Most would also agree that the mature professionals with whom student affairs practitioners associate and work, especially in their formative years and during transitional phases, can and do have significant influence on the quality and character of their professional development. Likewise, it is virtually assured that the mature professionals who influence those entering or advancing in the field, referred to as protégés, do so in diverse ways and for many different reasons. Sometimes the interaction that occurs is largely casual and informal in nature. The more mature practitioner may seek out or be called on by the less experienced individual to provide advice, consultation, or even instruction. These important, but usually informal, collegial, short-term, and sometimes supervisory relationships often tend to be task oriented in nature, focusing on a given event, problem, or issue. Consequently, much of the professional development that student affairs practitioners experience reflects individualized contact that occurs naturally in organizations with clear missions, where individuals are assigned varied responsibilities and others have expertise, knowledge, and previous experience that can be used to guide the implementation and maintenance of those responsibilities. There is little doubt that the resulting relationships can and do influence the behavior and character of evolving professionals. Conversely, many mature and committed professionals believe that it is important to provide special support on a continuing basis to those with less professional experience and maturity. The relationships established from interactions resulting from professional concern and desire to facilitate the professional development of others is often called *mentoring*, which is the focus of this chapter.

Mentoring as a Professional Developmental Process

From our perspective, principles of human development have direct application to professional development, and the mentoring process can and does facilitate the character of that development. Furthermore, we believe that it is possible to assess the impact of mentoring on the developmental experiences that influence the quality and character of student affairs professionals. Selected mentoring considerations are presented later in this chapter, as are the results of a nationwide professional development survey of student affairs professionals.

The professional development model proposed by Miller and Carpenter (1980) asserts that professional development exists as a parallel to personal development. It postulates the existence of four professional development stages (formative, application, additive, and generativity). Each stage represents a functional level of professional activity and behavior achieved via the accomplishment of relevant developmental tasks. This model was tested on several occasions (Carpenter, 1979; Carpenter, Miller, and Winston, 1980; Carpenter and Miller, 1981; Carpenter, 1991) and found to be useful for explaining the nature of professional development among student affairs practitioners. The model also postulated that mature professionals with whom individuals associate and work tend to function as primary influencers on that development in conjunction with exposure to the professional literature and other more impersonal modes of human communication.

Many student affairs professionals would argue that both personal, relatively intimate human interactions and impersonal, relatively cognitive and intellectual contacts are useful in professional development. However, there is little in the literature that explains the processes by which such activities influence professional development. The following discussion seeks to explain one important aspect of the professional development process and reports findings of a national study designed to enhance understanding of professional development in the context of student affairs practice. The authors contend that the more that is known about how and why student affairs practitioners develop, the more the profession can establish environments that are conducive to that development.

Findings obtained through the survey concerned the individuals, processes, and ideas that most significantly influenced development of professionals currently in the student affairs field. What personal, individualized developmental experiences had the greatest influence on the professional development of today's practitioners? Of particular interest were factors that influenced the formative, transitional years of professional development that ultimately lead practitioners to advanced stages. What factors influenced the mature professional to seek to give back something of value that clearly "makes a difference" by way of helping others to achieve their potential as student affairs practitioners? The primary significance of this study was to explore these important questions. Consequently, the role and function of mentoring became an important consideration.

Mentors and the Mentoring Process

The role of mentor and the function of mentoring have origins in Greek literature. In *The Odyssey,* when Odysseus' friend and adviser, Mentor, functioned as the king's son Telemachus's teacher while the father was abroad. Synonyms for *mentor* include the terms *teacher, coach, trainer, instructor, tutor, guide, friend, counselor,* and even *guru.*

The modern interpretation of *mentor* and *mentoring* typically calls for a somewhat spontaneous, usually informal relationship to exist between a more mature and experienced individual and one who is undergoing transition into a field of endeavor or to a more advanced level of responsibility within a chosen profession. It is during a period of transition when the need for mentoring is especially manifest and therefore is most useful.

Megginson and Clutterbuck (1995), in their book *Mentoring in Action,* make special note of the transition phase in their definition of mentoring, which is "off-line help by one person to another in making significant transitions in knowledge, work or thinking" (p. 13). Use of the "off-line" terminology suggests that mentoring is not usually considered an official responsibility of a line officer or primary supervisor, although those individuals may function as mentors from time to time. Rather, it is a relationship developed for purposes of aiding a less experienced staff member to "learn the ropes" in a new or different work situation. During times of transition, individuals tend to experience the greatest need for support and instruction. Such need influences both the establishment and the maintenance of mentoring relationships in professional work settings.

As in human developmental theory constructs, it is especially in times of life transition that individuals both are motivated to change and will seek support in that regard. There is a delicate balance between challenge and response when individuals are faced with previously unexperienced life circumstances. Those challenges tend to motivate individuals to action in attempts to resolve the disharmony they experience in their lives. Cognitive developmental theory (Piaget, 1965; Perry, 1970, 1981; Kegan, 1982) incorporates the constructs of cognitive dissonance, assimilation, and accommodation, whereas psychosocial developmental theory (Erikson, 1963, 1968; Sanford, 1967; Chickering, 1969;

Chickering and Reisser, 1993) makes reference to challenge, support, and response, all of which are pertinent to periods of life transition and discussions of growth and change. In effect, human developmental processes are at work in the development of professional student affairs practitioners, similar to the way they operate with cognitive and psychosocial development in individuals. When faced with life challenges, individuals typically focus psychic energy on resolving them and thereby lessening the dissonance between what they have previously been used to and what exposure to the altered environment imposes on them. Change tends to occur when individuals work through life challenges that demand accommodation if they are to develop and grow. The mentoring process can facilitate, and perhaps cushion, the essential changes that must occur for development to obtain.

Benefits to Mentors and Their Organizations

Although mentoring is no panacea—it cannot ensure the healthy professional development of all who experience it—the process has multiple benefits to those who mentor and their employing institutions and also to the protégés who receive mentoring. Mertz, Welch, and Henderson (1990) identify six benefits for the mentor and three benefits for the organization that are worthy of consideration. They contend that those who function as mentors benefit personally and professionally because mentoring

- Makes the mentor feel good (satisfaction gleaned from helping others)
- Makes the mentor look good (as being able to facilitate and encourage the professional development of others)
- Supports the mentor's image as a visionary (as a result of thinking of and systematically preparing for the future)
- Demonstrates what the mentor values (models behavior that signals that quality performance)
- Pays dividends (builds networks that provide support and access to information that was previously unavailable and promoting loyalty of protégés)
- Opens channels of communication (establishes open and honest relationships with others, who will ultimately provide an upward flow of communication)

Mertz, Welch, and Henderson (1990) further suggest that organizational perpetuation and renewal will result from the mentoring process in at least three beneficial ways. They contend that mentoring

- Builds a positive organizational climate (because of staff members learning about the organizational milieu, expectations, and work ethic)
- Provides a mechanism for rewarding staff members (as a result of participating in a sanctioned supervision strategy for those choosing to become so engaged)

- Builds a pool of ready talent (as a result of having a group of staff members whose talents have been both recognized and tested prior to consideration for promotion)

These and other benefits should provide chief student affairs officers, department heads, and other organization leaders with a rationale for encouraging and even establishing mentoring programs for new staff members or those facing transition situations such as being promoted, transferred, or reassigned. There is reason to believe that leaders who establish systematic mentoring programs will be rewarded with higher staff morale, greater staff loyalty, and more productive staff members than their counterparts who either resist or view systematic mentoring as unimportant. Although a mentoring relationship may last only a few weeks or months, the benefits to the program, the protégé, and the staff are significant, if largely incalculable. For most of us, it takes only a recollection of the stress and anxiety experienced when we were last faced with entering a new position or being assigned a major responsibility with which we were unfamiliar to realize the importance of mentoring support. If for no other reason, mentoring benefits organizations by better ensuring that all staff members are comfortable, knowledgeable, and confident in their ability to carry out their tasks with dispatch and efficiency and that they have easy access to a knowledgeable colleague who can provide help and support when required.

Benefits to Protégés

A recent mentoring meta-study by Bruce (1995) reviewed the findings of previous studies and identified several important mentoring consequences. Bruce pointed out that "despite lack of a specific operational definition of mentoring, research to date has provided indirect support for benefits of mentoring. Across the academic and business worlds, researchers cited mentoring outcomes as increased effectiveness regarding (a) retention, (b) developmental gains, (c) competence, (d) satisfaction, (e) job acquisition, and (f) subsequent career advancements" (p. 140).

Many benefits to protégés who experience a quality mentoring process were gleaned from the survey results, presented later in this chapter. The benefits derived by staff members in transition suggest that mentoring can provide

- A significant professional relationship
- An exemplar to observe and emulate
- Exposure to an intimate professional relationship
- Opportunities to participate in important professional growth activities (as a result of having an ally with whom to collaborate and from whom to receive both guidance during activities and individualized feedback afterward)

- Challenging, growth-enhancing experiences (as a result of exposure to one who genuinely cares enough to challenge a protégé with hard questions, difficult tasks, and stimulating experiences).
- Interaction with a friendly, caring colleague
- Association with an enthusiastic, dedicated professional
- Exposure to an open and accepting professional relationship
- Opportunity to open dialogue on professional issues
- Enhanced self-esteem (as a result of experiencing a meaningful relationship with a significant other who is faithful, loyal, and truly devoted to one's professional progress)

Survey on Influences

The foregoing has discussed the conception, role, function, and benefits of mentors and mentoring processes in a professional student affairs work setting. A presentation of the methodology and results of a nationwide survey of student affairs practitioners concerning primary factors that influenced their professional development concludes the chapter.

Method. The survey was designed by the authors to collect data about the nature and characteristics of people who have had a significant impact on the professional development of student affairs practitioners. The research project was funded by a grant from the National Association of Student Personnel Administrators (NASPA) Foundation. Surveys were distributed to 25 percent of the NASPA membership ($N = 921$), excluding graduate students and new professionals (defined as those who had been in the field for less than two years). A total of 382 surveys were returned (41.48 percent). Of those, 365 (39.63 percent) were usable for the study. Demographic information about the participants is listed in Table 5.1.

Table 5.1. Demographic Variables

Variable	Number	Percentage
Gender		
Male	168	46.3
Female	195	53.7
Ethnicity		
African American	32	10.7
Asian American	9	3.0
Biracial	3	1.0
Caucasian	249	83.0
Hispanic, Latino	5	1.7
Native American	2	0.7
Highest Degree Earned		
Bachelor's	11	3.1
Master's	197	56.1
Doctorate	143	40.7

Table 5.1. Demographic Variables *(continued)*

Variable	Number	Percentage
Degree in Student Affairs or Related Area		
Yes	237	64.9
No	128	35.1
Current Position		
Chief student affairs officer	84	24.4
Associate/assistant VP/dean	51	14.8
Director or department head	92	26.7
Associate/assistant director	65	18.9
Program-level staff	35	10.2
Faculty member	17	4.9
Current Institution		
Public	232	64.8
Private	126	35.2
Doctoral granting/research	142	39.8
Comprehensive	126	35.3
Liberal arts	59	16.5
Two-year/technical	30	8.4
Small (less than 5,000)	118	33.7
Medium (5,000–10,000)	108	30.9
Large (over 10,000)	124	35.4
Primary Area of Responsibility		
Chief student affairs office	103	32.3
Housing and residential life	75	23.5
Academic advising	40	12.5
Campus activities	22	6.9
Career planning and placement	11	3.4
Counseling services	7	2.2
Judicial programs	7	2.2
Leadership development programs	7	2.2
Preparation program faculty member	7	2.2
Minority student programs	6	1.9
Research and evaluation	5	1.6
Admission programs	4	1.3
Fraternity and sorority advising	4	1.0
Learning assistance program	4	1.3
College unions	3	0.9
Health services	3	0.9
Commuter student programs	2	0.6
Financial aid	2	0.6
Student orientation	2	0.6
Alcohol and other drug programs	1	0.3
Disabled student services	1	0.3
International programs and services	1	0.3
Recreational sports	1	0.3
Women student programs and services	1	0.3

Study participants were asked to respond to the following definition for purposes of identifying individuals who especially influenced their personal and professional development:

> *Personal influencers:* people who have helped you develop a sense of who you are, personally and professionally, and how you view yourself as a student affairs practitioner. Personal influencers will tend to be people with whom you worked, spent professional time, or who provided you with supervision or mentoring. They may be institutional colleagues or professional colleagues through various organizations/associations. These are people with whom you may have developed a close working interpersonal relationship.

Participants identified up to three personal influencers. Individuals most often identified were employment supervisors (55 percent), faculty members (18 percent), internship supervisors from graduate school (14 percent), colleagues or co-workers (8 percent), and professional association colleagues (4 percent). Participants as a whole tended to name more men than women as personal influencers, and women were more likely than men to identify women (X^2 = 8.27, df = 1, p = .004).

Participants were asked to list the words or phrases that best described the personal characteristics, work styles, ways of working with others, methods of modeling, and personal philosophy of each personal influencer. Table 5.2 shows the terms most commonly used by all the participants. Table 5.3 contains the responses given most often when respondents were asked to describe the nature and significance of their relationship to the personal influencer. It should be noted here that 93 (25.6 percent) respondents used the term *mentor* to describe the nature of their relationship with the personal influencer.

Table 5.2. Terms Used Most Often to Describe "Personal Influencers"

Term	Number
Compassionate	83
Role Model	55
Student centered	52
Empathic	51
Collaborative	41
Challenging	39
Personable	28
Enthusiasm for work	25
Open/Accepting	21
Devoted	19
Philosophical	19

Note: 161 other terms were cited 13 times or fewer.

Table 5.3. Terms Used Most Oftern to Describe the Significance of the Relationship

Term	Number
Mentor	93
Empowering	84
Encouraging	73
Empathic	40
Challenging	34
Attention to students	31
Compassionate	28
Good listener	16
Good teacher	14
Available/Accessible	11

Note: 137 other terms were cited 8 times or fewer.

Qualitative Responses. One of the earliest studies about the mentoring relationship was reported by Kram (1983). This study found that mentors serve two primary functions: providing career-related guidance and psychological support. Findings from Olian, Giannantonio, and Carrol (1986) support Kram's work but use the terms *intrinsic* and *extrinsic* to explain the aspects of the mentoring relationship. Bruce (1995) adds a third area, role modeling.

Respondents to the survey in this study were asked to describe specifically what it was about the personal influencer that made the relationship so significant and what this person actually did or said that made an important impact on their personal development. Although the authors of this study chose to subdivide the descriptive attributes into five areas, they represent qualities of guidance (personality traits and interpersonal behaviors), role modeling (leadership qualities and negative traits), and career support (career guidance and professional development).

Personality Traits. Many descriptors used by the respondents addressed specific personality traits that they viewed as important to the relationship. The terms included *spiritual, balanced, optimistic, empathic, passionate, honest, focused, flexible, ethical, intuitive, carefree, resilient, patient, nonjudgmental,* and *humble.* Following are descriptions given by several respondents:

- He was extremely supportive of all my endeavors. He emphasized standards of excellence.
- During the worst year of my professional life, she gave me honest and constructive feedback and unwavering support.
- She not only spoke up about social learning/social injustice, she also role-modeled and exemplified them in her personal and professional life.
- She has role modeled professional behavior in every way.
- He always brought out the fun in work and showed how humor had a place in even the most serious situations.

- She was compassionate and caring, yet firm. She was direct and had expectations that staff deal with each other in resolving conflict.
- He empowered us, inspired us to think big and make changes in an honest, ethical manner.
- He was always excited about new ideas and encouraged me to take a chance.
- She worked at and developed absolute trust. She presented challenges but shared, communicated, and empathized with us throughout every event.
- He believed in the balance of family and career. He encouraged me to believe that women could do it all and have it all if only they believed in their potential.
- She has achieved so much and yet is very gracious, humble, and genuine. She involved me, empowered me, and supported me even when she didn't need to and was busy with things on her own campus and in her own life.
- He is an eternal optimist who is hard driving and committed to finding effective ways of serving students. His persistence and optimism in this regard have taught me much in the way of working with people and projects.
- She is amazing in how she relates to students and is able to balance multiple responsibilities. I rarely, if ever, see her frustrated or stressed.
- He is my mentor. He consistently modeled ethical behavior and concern for people.

Interpersonal Behaviors. Many of the respondents discussed their personal influencer with regard to the treatment they had personally received from that person. These terms included *challenging, friend, direct, allowed mistakes, great teacher, gave responsibility, encouraging, accepting, unconditional support, empowering,* and *mentor.* Responses related to this category included the following:

- He articulated my strengths and weaknesses in a way no one had done before. I was supported to *try* rather than just *do* what I knew would be successful.
- She always treated me as an equal.
- She challenged me to confront my own biases and stereotypes.
- He made me feel important and valued as a colleague. He taught me how to behave professionally.
- He empowered me to make mistakes or succeed on my own merits, helped me understand the political dimensions of my work. He helped me be more open to change.
- She spent a significant amount of time with me and provided opportunities for leadership. She treated me as a whole person.
- She helped me formulate goals for myself.
- He had faith in my abilities as a young professional, encouraged me to grow, and was always willing to consider my suggestions.

- He was always challenging me to go beyond myself. I heard, "Yeah, but . . ." probably more times than I care to remember, but it always made me be solid in my thoughts and convictions or caused me to rethink my position.

Leadership Qualities. With so many participants naming supervisors as personal influencers, it is not surprising that leadership qualities were often cited. Specific leadership skills or traits that were given as reasons that individuals were viewed as influential included *policy setting, networker, financially astute, motivator, knowledgeable, problem solver, intentional, understands organizations, excellent supervisor, work ethic, politically aware, visionary, leader,* and *consensus builder.* Comments included the following:

- She collaborated on issues. Spent time analyzing processes, examined culture, structures, and governance.
- She took over a new office, giving it direction and organization while having time for family, friends, and colleagues.
- She created a work environment that supported collaboration. She was supportive but confronted behaviors and challenged assumptions. She protected the staff in difficult situations.
- Just watching her interact with both political and student affairs professionals, she is an artist at dealing with people.
- He taught me administrative skills, modeled high integrity. He involved me in staff meetings.
- He built collegiality among the troops and took away the need to compete to upstage others. He built a loyal following.
- He literally spent hours with me helping me understand the "corporate culture" of higher education.
- He believed that people come first and we can accomplish much and gain great achievements, but we must keep students and colleagues central to our goals.
- He led by example. He removed any perceived barriers fabricated by differences in levels of positions (job status).
- She created a work environment that was challenging and nurturing to empower me to rise to my potential.
- He truly loves work! He views each day as an opportunity to help students achieve their life goals.
- He was a good negotiator and taught me how to deal with negative situations immediately.
- He was a visionary. He was able to identify the heart of the issues.

Negative Traits. Many of the respondents identified a personal influencer who had a negative influence on their professional development. Negative role-modeling could have occurred through the manner in which they were personally treated or through observation. Specific traits mentioned included *unorganized, not sharing credit, disrespectful, sexist, sarcastic, used people, no scruples, disruptive, controlling, dysfunctional, chemically dependent, difficult,* and *co-dependent.* Comments from the participants included the following:

- She lied! The sad part is that we all knew she was lying. Yes, it was sad to watch a perfectly competent woman lie to your face.
- I learned some aspects of supervision that would have been inappropriate for me to try. I watched his style very closely and decided not to replicate it.
- This person helped me realize that I do not want to micromanage. I saw first-hand the negative outreaches [sic] of such a philosophy.
- I learned more of what I didn't want to be through him. However, this knowledge I believe is much more significant than merely attempting to emulate someone.
- She has not been an advocate for improvements within the department. She is mostly concerned with "covering my butt" as she states often. She does not inform her supervisees of decisions she has made that directly affect them.
- He taught me about the kind of supervisor I never want to be. He caused burnout in others by creating double standards, not allowing any time off, and creating problems for staff and students rather than solving them.
- She played favorites. Morale suffered tremendously.

Career Guidance and Professional Development. Most of the respondents listed one personal influencer who encouraged them to enter the field of student affairs or encouraged them to become professionally involved. Those individuals may be considered mentors, but the primary considerations listed pertain more to encouragement regarding career-related issues. For example,

- He took an interest in me and my professional development. He invested time, energy, and himself in me.
- As a new professional, she provided me with much insight and the motivation to continue in this field when it seems that the rewards just aren't enough.
- He encouraged and challenged my personal and professional development, recognized my potential, and helped me explore my professional choices.
- He took time throughout my employment to ask about my progress on developing professional goals. He even funded my registration for a professional conference the semester I was graduating and introduced me to many professionals and potential employers there.
- He encouraged me to get a Ph.D. and allowed me to maintain active involvement in professional activities/associations.
- This person shaped me as I evolved into a professional.

Concluding Comments

Four primary issues evolved from the data: gender issues, role of negative mentor traits, caveats for the term mentor, and formal programs.

Gender Issues. Although more men than women were identified in this study as respondents' personal influencers, previous research exploring gender differences in the mentoring process have produced contradictory results. For example, one study finds that women provide greater psychological support to protégés than do their male counterparts, whereas the latter provide more career guidance (Burke, McKeen, and McKenna, 1990). On the other hand, Struther's (1995) research indicates that organizational rank proved to be of greater importance than gender to the perception that women mentors are more concerned with psychological aspects than men are. More longitudinal research, such as the study by Orpen (1995), is needed to provide greater insight into the role of gender in the mentoring process. The initial findings of Orpen's research indicate that "the amount of vocational mentoring, but not personal mentoring, received by the participants during the first few months of their employment was associated with greater career success in the same organization over the next 4 years" (p. 668).

An area of concern for both mentor and protégé in cross-gender relationships concerns dual relationships and perceived public image difficulties. Cross-gender relationships are often stressful because of anxiety about intimacy and physical relationships (Clauson and Kram, 1984). Even when intimacy is not an issue in the relationship, the potential appearance of such can cause problems for both individuals. Comparable difficulty can exist in situations of dual relationships in which the mentor and protégé relate to each other in varied roles, often with unequal status as a variable. As Bowman, Hatley, and Bowman (1995) write, "no clear guidelines exist in the area of mentoring and social interaction regarding what constitutes a dual relationship or to what degree these may be a problem" (p. 233). In effect, cross-gender mentoring relationships are fraught with potential problems, especially in regard to organizational climate and societal values and expectations.

Role of Negative Mentor Traits. A number of the respondents who identified negative influencers indicated that sometimes we learn what we do *not* want to be by observing those around us in much the same way that we learn behaviors to emulate. Terms such as *micromanager, sarcastic, sexist,* and *chemically dependent* are not typically behaviors or attitudes that practitioners want associated with them, and yet the respondents expressed that they had in fact *learned* from observing that these were traits they did not want to acquire.

Caveats for the Term *Mentor.* Earlier in this chapter we mentioned that the term *mentor* is used today to denote a relationship that is much less formal, ongoing, and developmental than the term original users intended. For example, "peer mentoring" programs are often established to assist students in transitions to new experiences. In truth, peer mentors are of equal status, but they have some additional knowledge, expertise, or additional experience and serve more as advisors or guides. Levinson, in *The Seasons of a Man's Life* (1978, pp. 97–98), says that "the mentoring relationship is one of the most complex, and developmentally important, a man can have in early adulthood. . . . No word currently in use is adequate to convey the nature of the relationship. . . . words such as 'counselor' or 'guru' suggest more subtle meanings, but they have other connotations that would be misleading. The term 'mentor' is generally used in a much narrower sense, to mean teacher, advisor, or sponsor. . . . Mentoring is defined not in terms of formal roles but in terms of the character of the relationship and the function it serves."

Given Levinson's definition, it is doubtful that many of the respondents in this survey were truly referring to a mentoring relationship, when so few people have truly experienced that depth in their influential relationships. It might be better for student affairs practitioners to use terms that more clearly define the intended relationship type when establishing formal programs for new employees as part of their staff development programs.

Formal Programs. The findings in this study and previous research suggest that perhaps the most important, direct role taken by personal influencers is to provide career guidance and psychological support to junior employees. As discussed by Winston and Creamer earlier in this sourcebook (Chapter Three), the supervisory relationship is one in which these roles can be incorporated into the job function. However, formal programs, as part of a staff development plan, can ensure that all employees have the opportunity to benefit from an ongoing relationship with a senior staff member who is positioned and qualified to provide this type of guidance.

Some points to consider about such a formal program include the following:

- Assure individuals that program involvement is voluntary.
- Be aware of the positive characteristics of influencers described earlier in this chapter. Some individuals on the staff are not good candidates for such an important role.
- Provide training to those interested in working with junior employees so that all participants are operating from the same set of expectations.
- Consider having a time limit set for these relationships, even though the two people involved may choose to continue working together after the formal program has come to an end.
- Encourage both the more and the less experienced staff members to seek connections that will be mutually beneficial, and then let nature take its course.

References

Bowman, V. E., Hatley, L. D., and Bowman, R. L. "Faculty-Student Relationships: The Dual Role Controversy." *Counselor Education and Supervision,* 1995, 34, 232–242.

Bruce, M. A. "Mentoring Women Doctoral Students: What Counselor Educators and Supervisors Can Do." *Counselor Education and Supervision,* 1995, 35, 139–149.

Burke, R. J., McKeen, C. A., and McKenna, C. S. "Sex Differences and Cross-Sex Effects on Mentoring: Some Preliminary Data." *Psychological Reports,* 1990, 67, 1011–1023.

Carpenter, D. S. "The Professional Development of Student Affairs Workers: An Analysis." Unpublished doctoral dissertation, University of Georgia, Athens, 1979.

Carpenter, D. S. "Student Affairs Profession: A Developmental Perspective." In T. K. Miller, R. B. Winston, Jr., and others (eds.), *Administration and Leadership in Student Affairs: Actualizing Student Development in Higher Education* (2nd ed.). Muncie, Ind.: Accelerated Development, 1991.

Carpenter, D. S., and Miller, T. K. "An Analysis of Professional Development in Student Affairs Work." *NASPA Journal,* Summer 1981, 19 (1), 2–11.

Carpenter, D. S., Miller, T. K., and Winston, R. B. "Toward the Professionalization of Student Affairs." *NASPA Journal,* Autumn 1980, 18 (2), 16–22.

Chickering, A. *Education and Identity.* San Francisco: Jossey-Bass, 1969.

Chickering, A. W., and Reisser, L. *Education and Identity* (2nd ed.). San Francisco: Jossey-Bass, 1993.

Clauson, J. G., and Kram, K. E. "Managing Cross-Gender Mentoring." *Business Horizons,* 1984, 27, 22–32.

Erikson, E. H. *Childhood and Society* (2nd ed.). New York: Norton, 1963.

Erikson, E. H. *Identity: Youth and Crisis.* New York: Norton, 1968.

Kegan, R. *The Evolving Self: Problems and Process in Human Development.* Cambridge, Mass.: Harvard University Press, 1982.

Kram, K. E. "Phases of the Mentoring Relationship." *Academy of Management Journal,* 1983, 26, 608–625.

Levinson, D. J. *The Seasons of a Man's Life.* New York: Ballantine Books, 1978.

Megginson, D., and Clutterbuck, D. *Mentoring in Action: A Practical Guide for Managers.* London: Kogan Page Ltd., 1995.

Mertz, N., Welch, O., and Henderson, J. *Executive Mentoring: Myths, Issues, Strategies.* Washington, D.C.: U.S. Department of Education, 1990.

Miller, T. K., and Carpenter, D. S. "Professional Preparation for Today and Tomorrow." In D. G. Creamer (ed.), *Student Development in Higher Education: Theories, Practices, and Future Directions.* Washington, D.C.: American College Personnel Association, 1980.

Olian, J. D., Giannantonio, C. M., and Carrol, S. J. "Manager's Evaluations of the Mentoring Process: The Protégé's Perspective." *Proceedings of the Midwestern Academy of Management,* 1986, 143–148.

Orpen, C. "The Effects of Mentoring on Employees' Career Success." *The Journal of Social Psychology,* 1995, 135 (5), 667–668.

Perry, W. *Forms of Intellectual and Ethical Development in the College Years: A Scheme.* New York: Holt, Rinehart, and Winston, 1970.

Perry, W. "Cognitive and Ethical Growth: The Making of Meaning." In A. W. Chickering and Associates, *The Modern American College: Responding to the New Realities of Diverse Students and a Changing Society.* San Francisco: Jossey-Bass, 1981.

Piaget, J. *The Moral Judgment of the Child.* New York: The Free Press, 1965.

Sanford, N. *Where Colleges Fail.* San Francisco: Jossey-Bass, 1967.

Struther, N. J. "Differences in Mentoring: A Function of Gender or Organizational Rank?" *Journal of Social Behavior and Personality,* 1995, 10, 265–272.

DIANE L. COOPER is assistant professor and coordinator of the College Student Affairs Administration Program at The University of Georgia, Athens. She has served as NASPA Region III Research and Program Evaluation chair, on the Commission XII Directorate (Program Preparation Faculty) for American College Personnel Association (ACPA), and as president of the North Carolina Association for Women in Education.

THEODORE K. MILLER is professor emeritus of Counseling and Human Development Services at the University of Georgia, Athens, where prior to his retirement he was head of the department of Counseling and Human Development Services and coordinator of the Student Development in Higher Education Preparation Program within the College of Education School of Professional Studies. He has been actively involved in student affairs practice and graduate education for over forty years.

Self-reflection is an important component of the personal and professional development of those in student affairs.

Using Self-Reflection for Personal and Professional Development in Student Affairs

Joanne E. Nottingham

At the college and university level, human resource departments have long offered professional development workshops and seminars. In addition, faculty are becoming more formally engaged in the professional development process through "centers for teaching excellence" and the like. Divisions of student affairs, however, remain unique entities within colleges and universities because of staff involvement in the social and academic lives of students.

For this reason, the role of self-reflection should be considered an enhancement of traditional professional development efforts. This consideration of self-reflection is served by an understanding of one's personality, learning, and behavioral styles through the use of the following standardized instruments: the Myers-Briggs Type Indicator (MBTI); the Dunn, Dunn, and Price Learning Styles Inventory (LSI) for adults, known as the Productivity Environmental Preference Survey (PEPS); and the Carlson Personal Profile System (PPS). This chapter explores the role of self-reflection as an enhancement of traditional staff development efforts and reviews instruments that can help in understanding how personality, learning, and behavioral styles can aid self-reflective thinking and influence the effectiveness of student affairs professionals.

Using Self-Reflection

Self-reflection allows one to identify strengths and limitations in specific environments and the individual personality, learning, and behavioral characteristics that influence one's interactions with others. Other important aspects of self-reflection are the considerations of differing attitudes, beliefs, cultures, ethics, values, and life experiences. If professional development is essential to the effectiveness of departments and divisions of student affairs, then all staff members, from the newest employee to the chief student affairs officer, must have a meaningful understanding of themselves to maximize their individual effectiveness in the department or division. This examination of styles for the student affairs professional serves to assist him or her in understanding which traits and characteristics allow for the most effective interaction with others.

The case for self-reflection in student affairs is a powerful one. Effectiveness is an operational goal. Links to self-reflection in academia are often indirect and stated in terms of interdepartmental mentoring and fostering relationships with students. In corporate environments, effectiveness as a core component of leadership has been documented by best-selling authors Bennis and Nanus (1985) and Covey (1989). These authors rely on some elements of self-reflection in their explanations of leadership and how leaders can be more effective. Kouzes and Posner (1993) speak of leadership as a challenge that is dependent on the importance of perceptions of credibility; learning about oneself is key. Many authors (Cronin, 1993; Kelley, 1993; Morrison, 1993; Rosenbach, 1993) offer substantial support for the benefits of self-reflection for leaders from a variety of business perspectives.

Supporting the case for self-reflection in student affairs is the fact that characteristics of leadership are just as valid for professional development in academia as they are in corporate environments. The focus on the customer in most businesses is, for colleges and universities, more accurately a focus on the roles of in loco parentis, student services, and student development (Delworth, Hanson, and Associates, 1989). The effect of colleges and universities on students has been thoroughly examined by Pascarella and Terenzini (1991) in terms of the students' personal and interpersonal growth. Each college and university serves in one or more of these provider roles for each class of students it admits. For traditional students, the institutional roles are flexible in terms of recognizing and accommodating the primary changes in psychosocial development occurring at this time: self-concept, self-esteem, and identity, as well as the accompanying secondary changes in ethics, values, and morals. These changes in psychosocial development occur simultaneously with changes in the development of intellect. For nontraditional students, institutional roles are equally flexible, because a delayed return to school may be characterized by reexamination of self-concept, self-esteem, and identity. To a sizable degree, however, the issues of ethics, values, and morals have a minimal impact on this group of students.

Each student affairs department has a unique role in the lives of students at particular times during their academic careers. For example, admissions officers and orientation staff have direct and extremely meaningful relationships with first-year students. Career service employees initiate relationships with first-year students that the students may not consider important until their third, fourth, or fifth years. Psychological counselors provide services to students before or at the time they enter the university, and they also provide services to students who need them during their university years. Different relationships exist in each instance. Relationships between student groups or organizations and employees in the many student activities areas (student government associations, fraternities, sororities, and student organizations) are as varied as the groups or organizations. In these departments, staff effectiveness is tied to student–staff relationships via the type and intensity of communication created. Student affairs professionals, at some time or another, either directly or indirectly serve as "parents," provide services, and foster development.

The bottom line is that effectiveness in student affairs can be measured by how well programs and services are received by students. Effectiveness is dependent on the relationship between a specific department and the groups of students it serves. What does all this mean in terms of the professional development of student affairs staff? It indicates the importance of understanding our influence on students, what we represent in our student affairs positions and as people.

College and university graduate programs have provided a common academic knowledge base for student affairs staff members through master's or doctoral degrees. The experiential knowledge of staff, however, is as unique as each individual, because it is influenced by age, gender, marital status, ethnicity, religion, and institutional location and size, among other factors. Through attendance and participation at seminars, workshops, and conference meetings, new information is added to the academic and experiential knowledge bases, after which the information and experiences are analyzed, examined, and incorporated into the existing professional theory, recreating the theory in the process. Professional theory is active rather than passive, frequently changing as previously unknown information is learned and as new experiences occur.

Understanding Self-Reflection

Self-reflection can be defined in terms of critical or reflective thinking. It is the process of thinking critically about practice to develop theory, the development of expertise or control over professional actions combined with learning from experience (Russell, 1993). Specifically, the development of a professional theory appropriate to one's growth evolves from the use of skills for thinking critically about one's academic knowledge and professional experiences. To understand the concept of self-reflection, definitions and explanations from two perspectives are necessary: reflection, or reflective thinking, and critical thinking.

Reflective Thinking. Killion and Todnem (1991) define reflection as "the practice or act of analyzing our actions, decisions, or products by focusing on our process of achieving them" (p. 15). They note that Donald Schön offers two types of reflection: "*Reflection-on-action* is reflection on practice and on one's actions and thoughts, undertaken after the practice is completed. *Reflection-in-action* is reflection on phenomena and on one's spontaneous ways of thinking and acting in the midst of action. A third type of reflection, *reflection-for-action,* is the desired outcome" of the first two (p. 15). In other words, Schön looks at reflection in terms of reframing or "seeing a situation in a new way as a result of unexpected messages from practice" and new action or "a new approach to practice suggested by the reframing" (Russell, 1993, p. 53). Russell's interpretation of Schön's premises for the use of reflection in teacher education is very appropriate for professional development in student affairs, in that learning in both areas is a process of being told what to do, watching others, and doing.

For Dewey, "thinking is a postponement of immediate action . . . and the heart of reflection is the union of observation and memory" (1938/1963, p. 64). Periods of quiet reflection are considered so "only when they follow after times of more overt action and are used to organize what has been gained in periods of activity" (p. 63). Dewey's definition of reflective thinking considers actions in terms of problem finding and problem solving. He also stressed "the importance of anticipating future outcomes" (Bauer, 1991, p. 22) and that "planning ahead, taking notice of what happens, relating this to what is attempted are parts of all intelligent or purposeful activities" (p. 23).

Critical Thinking. The second perspective to assist in understanding self-reflection is critical thinking. Glaser (1941) defines it as "1) an attitude of being disposed to consider in a thoughtful way the problems and subjects that come within the range of one's experiences, 2) knowledge of the methods of logical inquiry and reasoning, and 3) some skill in applying those methods" (pp. 5–6). He sees critical thinking, which he also calls reflective thinking, as that which involves higher-order thinking or reasoning. This definition, with alterations, appears to be the basis of most other definitions. Ruminski and Hanks (1995) add the perspective that definitions of critical thinking tend to rely on sets of skills and should include some mention of the importance of attitudes or values. Their own offering of expert critical thinking skills includes the application, analysis, and evaluation of information and is not substantially different from Glaser's definition.

Nottingham (1997) defines critical thinking as disciplined thinking—a process of thoughtful analysis about an assertion to arrive at a conclusion or solution that is articulated by the thinker in words or by deeds. When one thinks critically and the result is an articulation of deeds or a change in behavior, the individual is a reflective practitioner in his or her field. Because critical thinking is logical, objective, and dependent on a philosophy of knowing, it is helpful in the critical thinking process to use a set of skills, even though these skill sets vary in number according to the source. Besides those noted, researchers such as Jones and Ratcliff (1993); Morgan (1995); Paul (1993); Potts (1994); and Zeidler, Lederman, and Taylor (1992) have offered lists of sets, as well as definitions, for review. Robert Ennis (personal communication, July 1996), a researcher of critical thinking, expands the context beyond skills or abilities and includes dispositions of critical thinkers.

Lists of critical thinking skills include such items as identification of main points or issues in the material, recognition of relevant or irrelevant information, recognition of verifiable or unverifiable information, investigation of inconsistencies, formulation of appropriate questions, separation of facts from opinions, and discernment of stated and unstated assumptions, biases, and stereotypes. The importance of critical thinking and its requisite skills is relevant for those working in student affairs, because understanding the role and applying the skills is beneficial not only to the professional but also to the student. An assessment must be conducted as to whether good communication exists between the staff member and the student, because interaction is a primary measure of effectiveness in student affairs. Student affairs professionals must combine academic knowledge and professional experience by developing critical thinking expertise to facilitate self-reflection for professional development.

Use of Selected Inventories in Student Affairs

The three inventories described measure specific style preferences and help define how each preference affects a person's interactions with others. Personality type preference is described by the Myers-Briggs Type Indicator (MBTI) (Consulting Psychologists Press, 1988); learning style preference is described by the Dunn, Dunn, and Price Learning Styles Inventory (LSI) for adults, known as the Productivity Environmental Preference Survey (PEPS) (Dunn, 1990); and behavioral style preference is described by the Carlson Personal Profile System (PPS) (Carlson Learning Company, 1996). Each of the inventories indicates the consistency of apparently random patterns in one's personal or professional life. They also share the common goals of improved self-understanding and more effective communication for those who use them.

Myers-Briggs Type Indicator. The Myers-Briggs Type Indicator (MBTI) of personality style (Consulting Psychologists Press, 1988) offers detailed explanations of sixteen personality types based on the combination of the strengths of four personality types: Sensing (S), Judging (J), Intuition (N), and Perceiving (P). The types are determined by using a combination of the four scales indicated:

- *Extroversion–Introversion (EI)*. This scale measures a preference for interest in people and things and ideas and concepts.
- *Sensing–Intuition (SN)*. This scale measures a preference for using the facts and reality of information and for considering possible meanings and relationships when examining it.
- *Thinking–Feeling (TF)*. This scale measures a preference for using judgment that relies on logical order and objectivity and that which relies on personal feelings and values and subjectivity.
- *Judgment–Perception (JP)*. This scale measures a preference for systematic planning and organization and for curiosity, flexibility, and spontaneity.

A better understanding of personality type allows the student affairs professional to capitalize on the multiple environments of student affairs in terms of attitude and intellect, and it allows the person to reflect on how he or she processes information. Use of the MBTI by those in student affairs is "suited to increase self-awareness in order to get along with others more effectively. It is also used to identify the source of problems in relationships . . . and to prepare a . . . plan for growth and change" (Kragness and Rening, 1996a, p. 6).

Student and staff characteristics of gender, economic status, race, and religion may be the same, yet problems may develop as a result of contrasting MBTI types, whereas students or staff members with the same characteristics and a complementary MBTI type may not have any problems. In the first situation, for example, the career services staff member with a strong type T (thinking), who bases decisions on logic and objectivity and works with a student or fellow staff member with a strong type F (feeling), who bases decisions on values and subjectivity, will likely have a difference of opinion with that student or staff member. In another example, a person with an MBTI type E prefers extroversion and one with and MBTI type I prefers introversion, so when a type-E residential life staff member interacts with a type-I student, a lack of communication is likely. Staff members with these opposite types are also likely to experience a lack of communication or difference of opinion.

Learning Style Inventory/Productivity Environmental Preference Survey. The Learning Style Inventory/Productivity Environmental Preference Survey (LSI/PEPS) model of learning style (Dunn, 1990) benefits people by offering explanations of how learners "concentrate, process, and retain new and difficult information" (p. 224). Communication is a crucial characteristic of interactions among student affairs personnel, and between them and the students they serve, so this type of information is particularly valuable. The acceptance of learning style as a useful concept in K–12 education has been expanded to teaching and administrative environments at the postsecondary level. In recent years, components of learning styles, often with different names, have appeared in many human resource and total quality management programs in colleges and universities. The LSI/PEPS model (Dunn, 1990, p. 225) measures the degree to which learners are affected by the factors of

- their immediate environment (sound, light, temperature, furniture and seating designs)
- their own emotionality (motivation, persistence, responsibility—conformity vs. nonconformity—and the need for either externally imposed structure or the opportunity to do things their own way)
- sociological preferences (learning alone, in a pair, in a small group, as part of a team, or with an authoritative or collegial adult and wanting variety as opposed to patterns and routines)
- physiological characteristics (perceptual strengths, time-of-day energy levels, and the need for intake or mobility while learning)
- processing inclinations (global/analytic, right/left, and impulsive/reflective)

A better understanding of learning style allows student affairs professionals to capitalize on their personal strengths when directing others and when teaching themselves. The nature of the LSI/PEPS model allows for the examination of individual multidimensional characteristics as a holistic and comprehensive way of understanding one's inclinations toward learning.

The use of the LSI/PEPS model by student affairs staff assists them in "learning and remembering better and enjoying learning more when they are taught through their learning style preferences" (Dunn, 1990, p. 239). It is obvious that in workshop, seminar, or conference environments consideration of the factors of the LSI/PEPS model is useful for professional development. If student affairs staff are engaged in a workshop that is scheduled just before lunch on a Thursday or Friday morning, impaired learning is a valid concern. If the temperature in the room being used for the workshop is too hot or too cold for the participants, impaired learning may result. If the workshop facilitator goes through the materials and tasks without allowing time for the participants to reflect, impaired learning is likely, unless some of workshop design has been for impulsive responses to activities. We all learn better when we are motivated and comfortable in our environment, when our energy level is high, and when we are not distracted by physiological needs such as hunger. Understanding and consideration of these and other characteristics are gained through a learning style model such as the Learning Style Inventory/Productivity Environmental Preference Survey.

Personal Profile System. The Personal Profile System (PPS) of behavioral style (Carlson Learning Company, 1996) benefits people by offering explanations of how and why people work more effectively with some than with others. The PPS instrument is a relevant and valid means to measure the impact of behavior on the learning of faculty, staff, and students. The specific dimensions of focus in the PPS are

- *Dominance (D)*. This dimension emphasizes shaping the environment by overcoming opposition to accomplish results.
- *Influence (I)*. This dimension emphasizes shaping the environment by influencing or persuading others.
- *Steadiness (S)*. This dimension emphasizes cooperating with others to carry out the task.
- *Conscientiousness (C)*. This dimension emphasizes working conscientiously within existing circumstances to ensure quality and accuracy.

A better understanding of PPS behavioral style allows the student affairs professional to capitalize on his or her behavioral strengths and increase his or her appreciation of those who have a different profile. It also allows them to have the capability of anticipating and minimizing potential conflicts with others. Strengths that are overused become limitations, so behavior is seen as something that is flexible and dynamic. As opposed to personality and learning style, particular behavior styles as indicated by the PPS are not preferred but serve as a means to recognize behavior and develop skills for more effective interaction with others. Recognition of behavior is different from recognition of personality in that those with differences in personality may have similarities in behavior. This incongruity may be tied to the fact that we all have different attitudes, beliefs, ethics, values, and life experiences that become a part of our core personality and affect our behavior. It is quite difficult to change personality, but, with assistance and time, a change in behavior is possible. The PPS is "primarily suited for increasing self-awareness in a setting where the individual can decide how to use the information in his or her relations with others" (Kragness and Rening, 1996a, p. 6).

Career services staff members who have a high D (dominance) dimension can encounter difficulties with students or staff, because their major goal is one of control and their major fear is lack of control. Under pressure, a staff member of this type can become domineering or impatient. If working with a student with a high I (influence) dimension, this staff member may risk the relationship, because such a student could have major fears of rejection and loss of approval and, under pressure, be likely to be disorganized and emotional. This situation hardly represents the optimal desired collaborative relationship when providing career services to students. The residential life staff member with a high D dimension would need to spend considerable time working on more effective means of communication with students who might view the control of the staff member as demeaning or threatening.

Interactions with students and staff members are affected by one's ability to overcome opposition to accomplish goals, one's persuasiveness, one's ability to cooperate and collaborate, and one's conscientiousness to quality and accuracy on the job. Greater or lesser strength in each of these areas has an impact on the student affairs staff member in terms of effectiveness and job satisfaction, and both are aims of professional development. Understanding and consideration of the characteristics we demonstrate to others are gained through the use of a behavioral style inventory such as the Personal Profile System.

There has been notable research supporting personality style's effectiveness and applicability in many professions (Briggs and Myers, 1983; Crockett and Crawford, 1989; Myers and McCaulley, 1985), as well as research on learning styles and their relationships with teaching styles (Borg and Shapiro, 1996; Dunn and Dunn, 1979; Grindler and Stratton, 1990). Research on behavioral style is limited and usually connected to research on personality. Kragness and Rening (1996b) note that limitations for the use of these style inventories are fairly consistent in that generalizations should be made with caution. Each style can be generalized to nonteaching environments if one is careful. It is better for the individual to generalize after consciously reflecting on experiences and connecting them with the present specific situation. In this context self-reflection is the conscious decision to discriminate and think about experiences and then link them with the current situation.

Enhancement of Professional Development in Student Affairs

The benefit of self-reflection for the growth and development of educators has been directly researched by a few and indirectly by many. Cranton (1996) provides support through a review of adult education literature. She specifically mentions Brookfield, Candy, and Mezirow as major contributors to building a theory of professional development "in which the complexity of self-directed learning is recognized, critical reflection is emphasized, and transformative learning is seen to be a goal" (p. xi). The use of the personality, learning, and behavioral style inventories discussed in this chapter contributes, in turn, to the components of this theory of professional development.

These inventories also help to answer some of Cranton's meaningful questions, such as how one learns about practice, learns to continue to grow and change, and learns to use reflection and understanding. Citing Habermas's research, Cranton (1996) distinguishes between several types of interests and knowledge: technical interests and instrumental knowledge that focus on predicting and controlling the environment; practical interests and knowledge that focus on the mutual understanding of the forms of social norms, traditions, and values in our culture; and emancipatory interests and knowledge that focus on the role of critical self-reflection for individual self-knowledge and social knowledge.

Concluding Comments

In summary, Cranton validates critical reflection as a key to learning from experience and determines it to be "the process in transformative learning" (p. 79). Mezirow (as cited in Cranton, 1996) states, "Adult development means the progressive realization of the adult's capacity to fully and freely participate in rational dialogue, to achieve a broader, more discriminating, permeable and integrative understanding of his/her experience as a guide to action" (p. 117). The author not only agrees with Cranton and Mezirow but also sees direct application of these findings to professional development in student affairs and believes that student affairs professionals increase and enhance their effectiveness and improve their professional development with the appropriate use of personality, learning, and behavioral inventories. Their use can benefit the development of theory, as well as practice, in student affairs.

References

Bauer, N. J. "Dewey and Schön: An Analysis of Reflective Thinking." Paper presented at the annual meeting of the American Educational Studies Association, Kansas City, Mo., 1991.

Bennis, W., and Nanus, B. *Leaders: The Strategies of Taking Charge.* New York: Harper & Row, 1985.

Borg, M. O., and Shapiro, S. L. "Personality Type and Student Performance in Principles of Economic Education." *Journal of Economic Education,* 1996, 27 (1), 3–25.

Briggs, K. C., and Myers, I. B. *Myers-Briggs Type Indicator, Form G.* Palo Alto, Calif.: Consulting Psychologists Press, 1983.

Carlson Learning Company. *The Personal Profile System.* Minneapolis, Minn.: Carlson Learning Company, 1996.

Consulting Psychologists Press. *Report Form for the Myers-Briggs Type Indicator.* Palo Alto, Calif.: Consulting Psychologists Press, 1988

Covey, S. R. *The Seven Habits of Highly Effective People: Restoring the Character Ethic.* New York: Simon and Schuster, 1989.

Cranton, P. *Professional Development as Transformative Learning: New Perspectives for Teachers of Adults.* San Francisco: Jossey-Bass, 1996.

Crockett, J. B., and Crawford, R. L. "The Relationship Between Myers-Briggs Type Indicator (MBTI) Scale and Advising Style Preference of College Freshmen." *Journal of College Student Development,* 1989, 30 (2), 154–161.

Cronin, T. E. "Reflections on Leadership." In W. E. Rosenbach and R. L. Taylor (eds.), *Contemporary Issues in Leadership.* Boulder, Colo.: Westview Press, 1993.

Delworth, U., Hanson, G. R., and Associates. *Student Services: A Handbook for the Profession.* San Francisco: Jossey-Bass, 1989.

Dewey, J. *Experience and Education.* New York: Macmillan, 1938/1963, in Dunn, R. S. and Dunn, K. J. "Learning Styles/Teaching Styles: Should They... Can They... Be Matched?" *Educational Leadership,* 1979, 36 (4), 234-244.

Dunn, R. "Understanding the Dunn and Dunn Learning Styles Model and the Need for Individual Diagnosis and Prescription. *Journal of Reading, Writing, and Learning Disabilities International,* 1990, 6 (3), 223–247.

Dunn, R. S., and Dunn, K. J. "Learning Styles/Teaching Styles: Should They . . . Can They . . . Be Matched? *Educational Leadership,* 1979, 36 (4), 234–244.

Glaser, E. M. *An Experiment in the Development of Critical Thinking.* New York: Teachers College, Columbia University, 1941.

Grindler, M. C., and Stratton, B. D. "Type Indicator and Its Relationship to Teaching and Learning Styles." *Action in Teacher Education,* 1990, 12 (1), 31–34.

Jones, E. A., and Ratcliff, G. "Critical Thinking Skills for College Students." Report no. R 117–G–10037. University Park, Pa.: National Center on Postsecondary Teaching, Learning, and Assessment, 1993. (ERIC Document Reproduction Service no. ED 358–772.)

Kelley, R. "How Followers Weave a Web of Relationships." In W. E. Rosenbach and R. L. Taylor (eds.), *Contemporary Issues in Leadership.* Boulder, Colo.: Westview Press, 1993.

Killion, J. P., and Todnem, G. R. "A Process for Personal Theory Building." *Educational Leadership,* 1991, 48 (6), 14–16.

Kouzes, J. M., and Posner, B. Z. "The Credibility Factor: What People Expect of Leaders." In W. E. Rosenbach and R. L. Taylor (eds.), *Contemporary Issues in Leadership.* Boulder, Colo.: Westview Press, 1993.

Kragness, M., and Rening, L. *A Comparison of the Personal Profile System and the Myers-Briggs Type Indicator.* Minneapolis, Minn.: Carlson Learning Company, 1996a.

Kragness, M., and Rening, L. *The Personal Profile System as a Measure of Personality.* Minneapolis, Minn.: Carlson Learning Company, 1996b.

Morgan, W. R., Jr. "Critical Thinking—What Does That Mean?" *Journal of College Science Teaching,* 1995, 24 (5), 336–340.

Morrison, A. M. "Leadership Diversity and Leadership Challenge." In W. E. Rosenbach and R. L.Taylor (eds.), *Contemporary Issues in Leadership.* Boulder, Colo.: Westview Press, 1993.

Myers, I. B., and McCaulley, M. H. *Manual: A Guide to the Development and Use of the Myers-Briggs Type Indicator.* Palo Alto, Calif.: Consulting Psychologists Press, 1985.

Nottingham, J. E. (ed.). *An Introduction to the Profession of Teaching: Critical Thinking Approaches.* Dubuque, Iowa: Kendall/Hunt, 1997.

Pascarella, E. T., and Terenzini, P. T. *How College Affects Students: Findings and Insights from Twenty Years of Research.* San Francisco: Jossey-Bass, 1991.

Paul, R. W. "The Logic of Creative and Critical Thinking." *American Behavioral Scientist,* 1993, 37 (1), 21–39.

Potts, B. "Strategies for Teaching Critical Thinking." Report no. EDO-TM–94–5. Washington, D.C.: ERIC Clearinghouse on Assessment and Evaluation, 1994. (ERIC Document Reproduction Service no. ED 385–606.)

Rosenbach, W. E. "Mentoring: Empowering Followers to Be Leaders." In W. E. Rosenbach and R. L. Taylor (eds.), *Contemporary Issues in Leadership.* Boulder, Colo.: Westview Press, 1993.

Ruminski, H. J., and Hanks, W. E. "Critical Thinking Lacks Definition and Uniform Evaluation Criteria." *Association for Education in Journalism and Mass Communication (AEJMC) Educator,* 1995, 30 (3), 4–9.

Russell, T. "Reflection-in-Action and the Development of Professional Expertise." *Teacher Education Quarterly,* 1993, 20 (1), 51–52.

Zeidler, D. L., Lederman, N. G., and Taylor, S. C. "Fallacies and Student Discourse: Conceptualizing the Role of Critical Thinking in Science Education." *Science Education,* 1992, 76 (4), 437–450.

JOANNE E. NOTTINGHAM is assistant professor of educational psychology and leadership studies in the Watson School of Education at the University of North Carolina at Wilmington. With many years of public relations and marketing experience in private-sector employment, she also serves as a private consultant in several professional development areas.

Training and staff development programs for student affairs constitute an investment in enhancing and developing skills for personnel in meeting institutional goals.

A Model for Staff Development in Student Affairs

Beverlyn Grace-Odeleye

This chapter provides a historical and current overview of staff development program models in higher education. It also traces the establishment of the Ball State University division of student affairs staff development program as a model in staff development design and functional program services. The chapter includes a discussion of past and present methods of evaluation processes, including the development of needs assessment questionnaires used in program development. Finally, the chapter discusses issues and trends and provides recommendations regarding emerging issues in student affairs for the twenty-first century.

Importance of Staff Development

In the past decade, college and university administrators have recognized the central role of staff development programs in accomplishing institutional goals. Student affairs professionals are now viewed as an integral part of the institutional mission. Cavalier and others (1994) noted that student retention activities often focus on the role of staff in interacting with students. Staff development is therefore imperative from a management perspective because it can have a positive effect on student welfare.

It is important that chief student affairs officers (or vice presidents) implement, sponsor, and support institutional staff development programs. In this regard, support for implementing comprehensive staff development programs should be supported philosophically and budgetarily. Supervisors must be concerned with the professional development of their staff; they should begin by involving all staff in identifying goals of a comprehensive professional development program (Bryan and Mullendore, 1990). The active commitments of chief student affairs officers in providing continuous training and education will pay dividends in personal growth and professional development for all staff. Staff members have an obligation to themselves and to their clientele to refine their skills, develop new responses to changing circumstances, and actively engage in their personal and professional growth. The continuing growth and development of student affairs professionals are a prerequisite for implementing a coherent and effective program of student development (Canon, 1980).

The staff development process includes formal and informal learning strategies for professional and personal growth. This process therefore plays a key role in helping staff in organizing and formulating appropriate staff development strategies to meet their needs (Bryan and Mullendore, 1990). Staff development programs indirectly assist in promoting institutional growth and development by providing tools and processes that allow staff to participate actively in formulating change through encouraging innovative ideas, approaches, research, and publication in professional journals. They also provide training related to job competency issues and develop managers who create a climate in the institution that empowers staff to help themselves (Price, 1988). Additionally, staff development programs can enhance staff abilities to understand and cope with rapid changes in institutional orientation, focus, funding, and demographics and thus redefine ways to provide good student affairs practices. A comprehensive staff development program serves to enhance student affairs staffs' effectiveness by improving specific staff skills that are requisite for achieving programmatic goals (Merkle and Artman, 1983). Such a program also provides new professionals the opportunity to improve their skill, competency, and confidence levels while contributing to the effectiveness of the institution. Canon (1980) described the rationale for staff development programs in student services in three common areas: the remediation and rehabilitation of marginally trained or skilled professionals, the enhancement of accountability to the institution for what one does as a professional, and the exercise of professional responsibility in the form of ensuring one's own continuing professional growth.

Common Elements of Staff Development Programs

Although the organizational structures of staff development programs differ from institution to institution, an examination of staff development programs at several institutions shows a common denominator. These programs are designed to provide necessary skill development and professional resources that engender personal and professional growth. Staff development programs representing a diverse spectrum of program services at the University of North Carolina at Greensboro, the University of Illinois at Chicago, Columbia University, and Ball State University are highlighted, reviewed, and discussed for their effectiveness. These programs are similar in their approaches and training areas but differ in institutional support.

In 1990, the University of North Carolina at Greensboro employee development program initiated training programs without including an organizational development component (Cavalier and others, 1994). Until the late 1980s, the human resources unit was a minor processing and record-keeping center with little opportunity to change the institutional culture. The vice chancellor for business affairs, responsible for program development in the office of human resources, realized the imperative of a well-versed and experienced student affairs administrative team. This idea led to a realization that the managers as presently trained were ill prepared for their supervisory assignments (Cavalier and others, 1994). Because of an increase in employee–management conflicts and complaints, complainants and other staff were included in the development of a new training program. This type of focused support developed into an advisory committee (Cavalier and others, 1994). The next step in the process of establishing an effective employee development program was to make explicit the university's commitment to the program.

During its early stages, participation in the program was voluntary. The effectiveness of the training experience was viewed as directly related to the degree of management support. Some specific concerns addressed were communication skills, supervisory skills, diversity concepts, problem solving, and dispute resolution. Program delivery to employees was through videotapes, case studies, modeling, role plays, and group processing, for example. According to Cavalier and others (1994), the program changed in 1992 from being problem-reactive to using an organizational development approach. Rather than merely being a vehicle for fixing specific problems on campus, the revised program was viewed as central to the educational mission of the university.

Cavalier and others (1994) describe the University of Illinois at Chicago training and organization development program that began in 1979 as a reaction to the needs of staff. Similarly to the University of North Carolina at Greensboro, the program was initiated in response to classified staff requests for training and development. An institutional needs assessment revealed the need for supervisory and management staff training and team building. The program training component was designed to meet the needs of four basic areas: management and supervisory training, staff development, management consulting, and organization development services (Cavalier and others, 1994). The aim of these functions was to change the campus organizational culture from one of intergroup competition to one of collaboration and empowerment. Topics covered in these programs included communication, conflict resolution, planning, and resource and time management. Management and supervisory training, consulting services, and unit interventions were assessed in several ways. According to Cavalier and others (1994), "The two of the most important are the degree to which the training, service, or intervention contributes to the improvement the unit sought and the dollar value of the improvement. The office of training and organization development attempts to focus the attention of clients and the campus on both the cost and the value of training and organization development services" (p. 63).

Columbia University's department of training and development program is a program encompassing a broad mission. Because of minimal staffing and budget allocations, creating a meaningful employee training and development program required creativity and resourcefulness. The key to the success of this program was building bridges to tap the resources in the university community. Relationships with faculty and administrators were cultivated to provide many leadership and employee development experiences at either minimal or no cost to the program and participants (Cavalier and others, 1994). The director of training and development decided what programs to offer and how to structure and deliver them. The program also benefitted from information received through informal benchmarking efforts with peer institutions that were more fully staffed and funded. Many programs and services were developed in response to direct requests from senior management for education on specific topics (Cavalier and others, 1994). A program needs assessment was used to assess the education or instruction priorities across the university. Some educational programs presented covered topics such as conflict resolution, team building, leadership development, supervisory training, and diversity-related issues.

Ball State University Student Affairs Staff Development Program Model

Ball State University is a public institution located in central Indiana. It has an enrollment of 18,500 students, with approximately 130 student affairs professional staff and 139 support staff in the division. The student affairs staff development program was formally started in 1976. Before the establishment of this program, there were staff development programs offered, but they were not systematically organized with clear focus and goals. In the early stages of the program, the associate dean of students realized that the purpose of an organized staff development program for the division of student affairs was the improvement and enhancement of personal and professional growth. The rationale for creating a staff development program (Canon, 1980) was defined as being to facilitate the personal and professional growth of individual staff members, to assist staff by promoting effective leadership in their positions and to assist them in achieving greater personal satisfaction from their work, and to help enhance the skills and competencies of new staff. The associate dean proposed these recommendations to the vice president for student affairs during the 1976–77 academic year. The vice president recognized and agreed that staff development was essential to increase the division's effectiveness in meeting the institution's overall mission. As a former president of the American College Personnel Association (ACPA), the vice president supported and understood the philosophy and need for professional development and realized that resources and financial support must be provided. The associate dean of students was assigned the duty of administering the program for professional staff at that time.

The associate dean of students established a divisional committee to implement the staff development program and also served as the committee chair, with representation coming from the different departments in the division. Committee members were appointed by department directors to serve one-year terms, with two at-large members appointed by the chair. The committee's responsibilities were (Beeler, 1977)

- To assess the needs and interests of the student affairs staff
- To plan a variety of programs in response to learned interests
- To coordinate professional growth activities for the total area
- To coordinate improved communication among the various areas regarding the ongoing programs and current concerns and issues
- To evaluate the offered growth experiences and make recommendations for future programs
- To arrange for the orientation of new student affairs personnel, through an introduction to the student affairs area and the university
- To provide in-service programming throughout the academic year and the summer

Since its inception, the program has undergone several adjustments in response to changing demographics. These changes were designed and determined by need areas, accomplishments, and future goals. The assistant to the vice president for student affairs is currently responsible for the staff development program.

An Evolving Program Design. Staff development programs that encourage flexibility and adaptation are essential for personal and professional growth. Program design has been the subject of much discussion and research in the last twenty-five years. Research supports certain strategies for planning, implementing, and designing a staff development program. Bryan and Mullendore (1990) stressed the importance of relating the goals of any professional development program to institutional mission statements. Staff development programs enable administrative units to be responsive to their stated missions and also to the needs of their constituent members. Successful strategies also include involving staff in the planning process and informing them of positive and negative outcomes. Comprehensive staff development programs that apply these strategies are more likely to produce well-trained staff who support the missions of the division and the institution.

Using these strategies, the Ball State staff development program committee examined the following questions before developing the program design:

- Are there particular programs or issues of interest to many staff?
- What benefit(s) should result: new knowledge, increased effectiveness, improved performance, and staff morale?
- What type of format is appropriate: workshops, small group discussion, or topical brown bag lunch sessions?
- Should the program be voluntary or mandatory?
- What are the available resources?

- Where does the committee find expert speakers and presenters?
- What is the budget and what are the costs and fees for speakers and refreshments?

During the first year of the staff development program, the committee presented two programs of interest. The "State of the Area Message" was presented by the vice president for student affairs, who discussed the new staff development program and the goals of the student affairs division. The second program (1976–77) included topics on emerging issues in student affairs that were of interest to managers. This program, titled "Legal Implications for Professionals," explored confidentiality, privacy restrictions, and affirmative action. In the second year of the program (1977–78) the priority for the committee was to conduct a needs assessment of individual staff interests. The needs assessment covered key program goals, objectives, issues, and diagrams designed to increase the effectiveness of managers and professional personnel. The assessment included type and design of programs (workshops or minicourses) of interest to staff, inclusion of experienced guest speakers in program activities, and a schedule for meetings to facilitate attendance. Results of the division needs assessment showed that student affairs personnel were interested in programs and activities in the following areas (Beeler, 1977):

- Leadership development (time management, personnel management, and decision making)
- Communicating effectively (writing reports and other professional documents and improving listening skills)
- Career planning (professional and support personnel)
- Needs of students with disabilities (understanding issues and how best to serve these students)
- Improving skills (use of technology, understanding today's business world, values clarification)
- Social activities (fostering positive relationships among student affairs staff)

The analysis and interpretation of the needs assessment resulted in planning and presenting programs that directly improved the quality of performance of student affairs managers. The scheduled programs were presented in workshop format, with continuing education units (CEUs) available. As a result of the needs assessment, the programs presented included programs to improve proficiency in the use of computer software, to improve service to students with disabilities, to aid staff interested in positions requiring increased responsibilities, to improve customer and human relationship skills, and to help staff discuss and explore their values.

During the 1978–79 academic year, a new-staff orientation workshop was carried out by the student affairs staff development committee. The purpose of the workshop was to acquaint new staff with divisional and institutional goals and with the campus and community as quickly as possible. In this process, new staff members met with the vice president, who discussed the philosophy, structure, and function of the division of student affairs and provided information about the campus and community culture.

A support staff development committee was formally started in the division of student affairs during the 1989–90 academic year. Before this time, the associate dean of students presented a program for the support staff each year that provided a "student affairs update" given by the vice president. A division committee was formed, with the associate dean as chair and representatives from all areas of the division. A needs assessment was administered, and the following workshops were presented, with CEU credits available for selected programs: stress management, writing skills for secretaries, employee benefits, interoffice visitations for the different areas, and brown bag lunches (forty-five-minute, short-topic programs). These programs were well attended by support staff.

The student affairs employee involvement program (EIP) was started by the division in 1990 with the purpose of improving the quality of service and promoting the involvement of all staff (management, support, service) in problem solving and prevention. Originally, the program was designed to encourage the active involvement of support and service staff working in teams to identify, research, and solve work-related problems in individualized areas in student affairs.

The program, under the leadership of the vice president for student affairs and the associate dean of students, included a steering committee responsible for organizing and monitoring the progress of the program, a facilitator who coordinated team and liaison training and progress, liaisons to the focus teams, and the focus teams, which identified problems or concerns in the individual areas.

In 1993, staff throughout the division of student affairs contributed to the EIP evaluation and improvement in many ways. An assessment survey was distributed to professional staff, focus team members, and the co-workers of focus team members to gather data to evaluate the strengths and weaknesses of the program and to assist in planning for future direction and improvements. As a result of the survey, the steering committee changed the program's name from the employee involvement program to the quality improvement program (QIP). Borrowing from the total quality management (TQM) model strengthened the program's focus on quality and provided the format for a working strategic planning document.

The philosophical principles of the quality improvement program were as follows (Association for Quality and Participation, 1991):

It's the system. Do not blame people; change the system. Quality improvement efforts focus primarily on examining work processes and evaluating their effectiveness rather than on assigning blame to the people doing the job.
Strive for constant improvement. Do not look for the quick fix; maintain constant pressure for improvement of the system.

Be part of a learning organization. Education and training are what sets a high-quality organization apart. An organization in which staff believe that improving themselves and the organization is part of their jobs is a dynamic, "learning" organization.

Use teamwork. Do not blame each other; work together. An organization that just follows orders is static, because it depends entirely on the ideas of a few people at the top. Teams of employees generate more and better ideas than individuals working alone, and the solutions put forward by teams are more quickly implemented and last longer because the people doing the job have contributed to finding ways to improve the job. Remember, "If you keep doing what you've always done, you'll keep getting what you always got."

Use data. Do not base decisions or recommendations for change on opinions; gather and use data to base decisions and recommendations on fact.

Build an attitude of problem prevention. Strive for problem prevention by anticipating needs and building processes and systems that work.

Manage the system, not the people. The supervisor's job is not to make people work but to improve the system. The worker's job is not to fight the system but to manage it.

Break down barriers between and within departments. Work together; communicate ideas and help one another.

Focus on quality. Educate yourself and use every ounce of influence you have to encourage others to educate themselves about how to provide quality service to internal and external customers. Quality is everyone's job.

Drive out fear. Listen to the suggestions of others; encourage communication.

People are the greatest untapped resource in the organization. People are the only asset within an organization that increases in value.

Empowerment. People rarely rise above the expectations set for them, but they will accomplish more than expected if empowered and supported in their desire to do so.

The program was instrumental in making not only division policy and procedural changes but institutional changes, as well. The vice president and others made several national presentations on this model. During the fall of 1995, a social component (a student affairs holiday social) hosted by the vice president was added to the staff development programming. This event presented an opportunity for staff members (management, support, and service) who did not normally interact, to get together for an evening of fun during the holiday season. Because families were invited, this was a well-attended, successful event.

The Jack Beyerl lecture series was started in April 1996 to recognize the support and contributions of Jack Beyerl to the Ball State University division of student affairs staff development program. Dr. Beyerl, former vice president for student affairs and dean of students for twenty-four years, was instrumental in creating the staff development program. This lecture series honors his commitment to staff development and the positive influence he had on the lives of many students. Each year a distinguished national speaker in student affairs or higher education is invited to share his or her research with the university. This successful, well-attended lecture series is supported by academic affairs and graduate and undergraduate students at Ball State University and higher education colleagues from around the state.

The student affairs awards and recognition program, started in 1996, recognizes outstanding contributions of student affairs staff to the division and to the university. The purpose of the program is to recognize the contributions of student affairs employees for their job commitment, exemplary performance, exceptional and dedicated service to students, and accomplishments above the call of duty. Staff are nominated for awards in the following categories: research; program/activities/customer service; graduate assistant and student employee; new management, service, and support staff; and management, service, and support staff. These awards have served to increase morale and foster a sense of pride in the services provided to students and the division. Recipients receive a monetary award to attend workshops, seminars, or professional conferences, as well as other recognition.

The staff development program has faced many challenges over the years, resulting in new priorities and changes in the division and the institution. Diminishing financial resources, issues of accountability in providing quality programs, and assessment of the ever-changing needs of staff are three primary challenges. The program is constantly evaluating and reviewing procedures for program selection in an effort to increase effectiveness, efficiency, and responsiveness to staff needs and interests.

Evaluation of Program. Originally, the staff development program needs assessment questionnaire was administered sporadically. During the first year and every two years after that, program evaluations were based on perceived need. Since 1990, the committee has assessed the professional and personal needs of staff through a yearly assessment questionnaire. The purposes of the needs assessment questionnaire are to assist the committee in planning and identifying staff development programs; to help in identifying divisional and institutional needs and to assist in ranking those needs; to aid staff in identifying, developing, and meeting professional and personal goals; to identify training needs based on the goals of the division and institution; and to identify attitudes about changes in new services, skills, and technologies.

Each program is evaluated by the reaction of participants at the conclusion of that specific program. Attendance at the program is also an evaluative tool in assessing interest and need. Finally, feedback from colleagues in individual areas serves as a form of evaluation in assessing need and in presenting specific skill workshops in individual areas.

Concluding Comments

Since the early 1990s the emphasis in higher education has been on accountability, efficiency, and results. This trend will continue into the twenty-first century as less financial resource allocations are available and the expectations for creating more efficient institutions of higher education continue. State legislators, boards of trustees, and higher education administrators will continue to focus on reducing costs while enhancing the delivery of quality services to all citizens. Student affairs divisions will be forced to examine creative alternatives to maintaining and supporting current and future staff development programs. The following recommendations are offered as a starting point for student affairs as we enter the next century. Student affairs administrators must

- Be creative in identifying financial support to fund staff development activities. Administrators must more actively pursue outside agencies in their quest for funding to support specific staff development needs.
- Seek opportunities to jointly sponsor programs with other institutional divisions and with academic and student affairs professional organizations. Common staff development needs exist across institutional administrative lines of authority.
- Investigate the option of contracting for or out-sourcing some types of programs and functions because of budgetary constraints.
- Seek resources to expedite the use of technology for distance learning (interactive capability) as a main delivery system for providing staff development. Costs associated with the use of technology can be shared within institutions.
- Use assessment and evaluation tools to intensify responsiveness to staff development needs and assess the effectiveness of delivery models.
- Provide a strong design model for staff development programs in such areas as consensus building, conflict resolution, and teamwork with students, parents, board members, and legislators in order to be responsive to constantly changing expectations.

In summary, increased accountability, efficiency, and results in the presence of reduced or diminishing budgets will require student affairs staff to be creative and to work with an array of external agencies in designing programs and providing services and internal resources.

References

Association for Quality and Participation. *Basic Facilitator Development Course: Coordinator's Notebook.* Cincinnati, Ohio: Association for Quality and Participation, 1991.

Beeler, K. D. "Staff Development in Student Affairs: The Referral Process." *NASPA Journal,* 1977, 15 (2), 14–23.

Bryan, W. A., and Mullendore, R. H. "Professional Development Strategies." In R. B. Young (ed.), *The Invisible Leaders: Student Affairs Mid-Managers.* Washington, D.C.: National Association of Student Personnel Administrators, 1990.

Canon, A. J. "Developing Staff Potential." In U. Delworth, G. R. Hanson, and Associates (eds.), *Student Services: A Handbook for the Profession.* San Francisco, Calif.: Jossey-Bass, 1980.

Cavalier and others. "Staff Training and Development Programs." In S. A. McDade and P. H. Lewis (eds.), *Developing Administrative Excellence: Creating a Culture of Leadership.* New Directions for Higher Education, no. 87. San Francisco: Jossey-Bass, 1994.

Merkle, H. B., and Artman, R. B. "Staff Development: A Systematic Process for Student Affairs Leaders." *NASPA Journal,* 1983, 21 (1), 55–63.

Price, G. "Developing Managers to Prevent Staff Burnout." In V. J. Marsick (ed.), *Enhancing Staff Development in Diverse Settings.* New Directions for Adult and Continuing Education, no. 38. San Francisco: Jossey-Bass, 1988.

BEVERLYN GRACE-ODELEYE is the student ombudsperson/assistant to the vice president for student affairs at Ball State University. She has worked in student affairs since 1981 and has held various positions designed to improve policies and quality services to students. She is a member of several professional organizations.

Most student affairs professionals would agree that staff development is of major importance to the student affairs profession in the twenty-first century.

Some Final Thoughts About Staff Development

William A. Bryan, Robert A. Schwartz

With the increasing demands from numerous higher education constituencies, educators can let their minds run wild as they contemplate changes to the campus culture in the twenty-first century. Central to the delivery of quality learning opportunities and services for students in the next century is an educated, energetic, motivated management and support staff in tune with the campus milieu and committed to the campus mission. In turn, campus environments must be supportive of the development of human capital, especially the staff recruited to carry out the mission of the university. Educators can bemoan the many barriers that challenge higher education and how such barriers inhibit commitment to staff development; regardless, they must be creative in identifying strategies to overcome the barriers that at times seem so ominous. We must spend money wisely, carefully examine how we conduct our work, and develop an extended view of how staff grow personally and professionally.

We view staff development as beginning in the recruitment process and extending through the life of staff to the point of retirement. This view encompasses an expanse of time and varying personal and professional needs of staff along a continuum. Our perspective also requires the development of shared vision by institutional leadership and personnel in identifying staff needs and interests at different points in a person's work life. Staff development can be broadly viewed as activities and programs (formal or informal and on or off campus) that help staff learn about their responsibilities, develop required skills and competencies necessary to accomplish institutional and divisional goals and purposes, and grow personally and professionally to prepare themselves for advancement in the institution or beyond the campus. Informal opportunities such as staff cookouts, dinners, luncheons, and recreational events can be beneficial in developing a sense of staff cohesion and working as a team.

In essence, campus leaders must be deeply concerned with the total growth of their staff members, and the dimensions of well-being that encompass a holistic view of the staff person. Quality creative communication that occurs between supervisor and employee must address the personal growth as well as the professional enhancement of a staff member, since growth in the personal realm will aid the staff member in her or his professional life. The question might be, Are these two functions really separate? The answer appears to be *no*.

This sourcebook has provided a discussion of important elements of personal and professional education that further growth and development for staff, including a discussion of relationships that are supportive of staff development.

Important Elements

As Harned and Murphy point out in Chapter Four, supervisors should explore with employees the skills needed to do a good job. If weaknesses in work performance are identified for employees, the supervisor has a responsibility to help them improve.

Growth Contract. An employee growth contract can be developed following a discussion between the supervisor and employee of the employee's interest in personal and professional growth (improvement of skills and abilities) over a set period. The contract is formulated regarding what is expected from the supervisor and also from the employee. As part of the annual professional development plan (PDP), the employee may negotiate with his or her supervisor a growth contract that identifies specific avenues that will help this staff person enhance knowledge, skills, ability, and attitude. Such enhancements can relate to personal, professional, or job growth (Mullendore and Wang, 1996)

Mentoring. In Chapter One, a mentor provides "a trusted relationship of guidance and advice." For the growth contract to be effective, a trusting relationship must exist. The employee must feel comfortable enough in the supervisor-employee relationship to risk and share personal and professional needs and interests. Cooper and Miller (Chapter Five) identify other synonyms for mentor—"teacher, coach, trainer, instructor, tutor, guide, friend, counselor, and even guru." A supervisor may be viewed as a mentor by some of his or her staff.

Synergistic Supervision. Winston and Creamer (Chapter Three) present their conception of synergistic supervision as "a helping process provided by the institution to benefit or support staff rather than as a mechanism for punishment inflicted on unsatisfactorily performing practitioners." Synergistic supervision, as defined, is crucial to an effective staff development program (see Winston and Creamer, 1997).

Relationships. Although the supervisor-professional staff relationship is extremely important, Harned and Murphy (Chapter Four) discuss five additional relationships that are critical in developing a climate for staff growth and development. These relationships include (1) profession-institution, (2) profession-staff, (3) profession-supervisor, (4) institution-supervisor, and (5) institution-staff. Attention to the development of positive, supportive, synergistic relationships in these six areas will enhance the potential for growth and development of the profession, institution, and staff.

Human Performance System. In Chapter Two, Holmes discusses a human performance system for student affairs. Through the implementation of this model in a division, a foundation is laid "for the continuous and appropriate development of" staff. "A greater sense of community" is developed in the organization, and "it provides a methodology . . . for student affairs practitioners to more effectively unite professional development and organizational effectiveness." Important components of this model are staff recruitment, selection, and retention; staff performance planning and goal setting; staff coaching, performance assessment, performance reward, and development; staff career planning, development, and transition; organization development; and diversity empowerment.

Self-Reflection. Basic to an optimum climate for staff development is a staff member's understanding of her or his personality and learning and behavioral styles. Nottingham (Chapter Six) believes that staff members "must have a meaningful understanding of themselves to maximize their personal effectiveness." She makes a strong case for the use of self-reflection in student affairs.

Comprehensive Program. Grace-Odeleye (Chapter Seven) provides historical perspective in the evolution of a comprehensive staff-development program in the division of student affairs at Ball State University. She shows that such a program serves to enhance staff effectiveness by improving skills, competency and confidence levels while helping a division of student affairs and university be more effective. She encourages a collaborative program that goes beyond university-division lines of authority.

Challenges

Although there are many ingredients that go into the development and achievement of an effective staff development program, we will focus on three important elements—the institution-division, the profession, and staff members.

Institution-Division. A major outcome of the personal and professional education of staff is a positive enhancement in organizational performance. Higher education leaders must provide the time, resources and philosophical commitment in staff development for institutional vision and mission statements to become a reality. First, there must be a collaborative spirit in the development of vision and mission statements and consensus regarding goals, core values, and desired campus culture. Second, institutions must seek and value staff who make capable decisions, set specific work standards and goals, organize their work, and relate positively to many customers. Third, leadership must invite staff examination, debate, and challenge to institution-division assumptions and beliefs by providing open forums for discourse. Fourth, programs and activities that help staff to anticipate and be responsive to needed change in new and innovative ways are an imperative if universities are to provide quality service for their many constituencies.

Of primary importance is the intentional development of comprehensive institution-division programs for staff development. Campus centers for staff and faculty excellence can be umbrella organizations to support the growth and development opportunities in university departments and divisions. Many common elements or needs for staff development programs are available whether a staff person is in a business affairs, student affairs, academic affairs, or a human resources setting. Partnerships across institutional boundaries must be rewarded. Finally, student affairs staff, like all university personnel, are present to aid students in their learning and development. Staff development is imperative because its outcomes exert a positive effect on student welfare.

Profession. The student affairs profession has long been committed to staff development. Staff development opportunities that relate to the general area of student affairs or specifically to members' work in student affairs specialty areas are offered annually by student affairs associations. These associations plan and implement national and regional workshops in response to member needs and interests.

The Council for the Advancement of Standards in Higher Education recently published *CAS: The Book of Professional Standards for Higher Education* (1997). This publication mentions, in a cursory manner, the importance of providing "appropriate professional development opportunities" for staff (p. 95). This statement is present in all functional area standards and guidelines published by the council. Nevertheless, a separate statement of staff development standards and guidelines for student affairs practice is essential at this time. Professional development standards of practice will promote more synergistic relationships among student affairs professionals and supervisors, the student affairs profession, and campus leaders.

Professionalization (for example, standards and licensure) and professionalism (for example, behaviors and actions) of our staff are important factors in the development and respect of our profession in the higher education community. Through convention programs, professional literature, and colleague discussions, student affairs professionals have frequently debated the issue of whether student affairs is a profession. Tantamount to being a profession is the establishment of licensure standards for members of a group, statements of expected practice, ethical standards, and so on.

Critical to the staff development of student affairs leaders is their strong connection and association with professional organizations. These organizations provide an easy entre for staff with similar interests to meet and work together, to become involved in areas of interest related to their campus work, and to gain a greater sense of the student affairs profession, its culture, and its past and future needs.

Staff Members. Professional behavior includes a staff member's being involved in her or his own growth and development. Personal and professional education begins in graduate preparation programs and extends throughout a person's professional life to retirement. Self-reflection assists staff in knowing who they are, what really motivates them, and what their strengths and needed areas of growth are. In short, staff must be actively involved in their own growth and development process.

As discussed in this sourcebook, the supervisor-staff relationship is a key ingredient of productive staff development. Staff members must commit to making staff development a priority. Their active involvement in programs and activities such as forums, discussions and debate; development of vision, mission, and goal statements (personal and institutional); solving problems; mentoring and other colleague-institutional relationships; growth and renewal activities; developing partnerships; and assessment of their performance are necessary for them to grow and develop as student affairs professionals and for them to have a positive effect on student welfare. As previously suggested, staff behavior will model appropriate behavior for students.

Concluding Comments

Personal and professional education take many forms in student affairs divisions and human resource departments across the country. Optimally, it is a process that leads to the development of quality professional staff and, in turn, to organizational effectiveness. As the twenty-first century unfolds, the provision of staff development opportunities for higher education employees is a necessary mandate. We must remember that our focus is to serve students. Therefore, the necessary tools, resources, learning opportunities, and philosophy that aid staff in providing needed student development and learning experiences should be provided.

An intentional delivery model for staff development is necessary for the optimum growth of staff and institutional response to vision, mission, and goal statements. The formation of a staff development delivery model must be a participative process including many institutional constituencies.

In summary, professional development takes place on different levels, in different settings, from individuals to national associations. It can be delivered in several ways—as a formal effort, through informal networks or activities, or as nonformal experiences such as observing or apprenticeships. It is important to consider what the use and value of professional development is and how it will be achieved in an organizational context. How is it to be used? Who will participate? What outcomes are expected? Understanding and considering each of these areas will make professional development efforts more successful and more effective. Staff development is too important to colleges and universities, campus constituencies, and students to be left to chance.

References

Bryan, W. A. "What Is Total Quality Management?" In W. A. Bryan (ed.), *Total Quality Management: Applying Its Principles to Student Affairs.* New Directions for Student Services, 76, San Francisco: Jossey-Bass, 1996.

Council for the Advancement of Standards in Higher Education. *CAS: The Book of Professional Standards for Higher Education.* Washington, D.C.: Council for the Advancement of Standards in Higher Education, 1997.

Mullendore, R. H. & Wang, L. (1996). In W. A. Bryan (ed.), *Total Quality Management: Applying Its Principles to Student Affairs.* New Directions for Student Services, no., 76.

Winston, R. B., Jr., and Creamer, D. G. *Improving Staffing Practices in Student Affairs.* San Francisco: Jossey-Bass, 1997.

WILLIAM A. BRYAN *is professor emeritus of education in the Watson School of Education at the University of North Carolina at Wilmington. He served as a chief student affairs officer for eighteen years and is past president of the American College Personnel Association (ACPA) and the ACPA Educational Leadership Foundation. He has been actively involved in student affairs practice for thirty-seven years.*

ROBERT A. SCHWARTZ *is associate professor of higher education and student affairs at Florida State University. He has been active in higher education as a faculty member and administrator for over twenty years.*

INDEX

American College Personnel Association (ACPA), 9, 20, 86; learning imperative of, 20
Artman, R. B., 6, 84
Association for Quality and Participation, 89

Baldridge, J. V., 9
Ball State University, 2, 83, 84
Ball State University, model for staff development, 86–87; staff development committee, 87; needs assessment, 89; employee involvement program (EIP), 89; support staff committee, 89; quality improvement program (QIP), 89; philosophical principles, 89–90; Jack Beyerl lectures, 90; student affairs awards and recognition, 91; program evaluation, 91
Barr, M. J., 9, 10, 11
Bassi, L. J., 15
Bauer, N. J., 74
Baumgartner, D., 45
Bayles, M. D., 12
Beeler, K. D., 5, 87, 88
Bennis, W., 72
Bergquist, W. H., 9, 10
Bhola, H. S., 8
Bilger, M. A., 17
Birch, J. W., 51
Birnbaum, R., 19
Blake, R. R., 31
Bolman, L. G., 9, 10
Borg, M. O., 78
Bowman, R. L., 67
Bowman, V. E., 67
Brennan, E. J., 21
Bricker, B., 16
Briggs, K. C., 78
Brookfield, Candy, and Mezirow, 79
Brown, S. S., 5, 19, 30, 36, 39
Bruce, M. A., 59, 63
Bryan, W. A., 1, 2, 3, 6, 83, 84, 87, 95
Bureau of Labor Statistics, 15
Burke, R. J., 67
Burke, T. H., 36

Callahan, M., 16
Canon, A. J., 84, 86

Canon, H. J., 6
Career anchors, 33–34; defined, 33–34; competence and, 34; job security and, 34; creativity and, 35; service and dedication, 35; autonomy, 35; challenges, 35; lifestyle, 36
Carlson Learning Company, 75, 77
Carlson Personal Profile System (PPS), 71, 75, 77–78
Carnevale, A. P., 15
Carnevale, E. S., 15
Carpenter, D. S., 37, 56
Carrol, S. J., 63
Cavalier and others, 83, 85–86
Chickering, A., 57, 58
Clauson, J. G., 67
Clutterbuck, D., 57
Cognitive developmental theory, 57
Cohen, M., 9
Columbia University, 84, 85
Columbia University, Teachers College of, 4
Consulting Psychologists Press, 75
Continuing education credit (CEU), 9, 88, 89
Coombs, P. H., 8
Coomes, M., 11, 12
Cooper, D. L., 2, 55, 96
Council for Advancement of Standards in Higher Education (CAS), 8, 98
Covey, S. R., 72
Coyne, R. K., 16
Cranton, P., 79
Crawford, R. L., 78
Creamer, D. G., 1, 2, 29, 30, 33, 36, 37, 68, 96
Critical thinking, 74
Crockett, J. B., 78
Cronin, T. E., 72
Culture and higher education, 9; types of, 9–10; symbolism in, 9–10
Curtis, D. V., 9

Deal, T. E., 9, 10
DeCoster, D. A., 5, 19, 30, 36, 39
Delworth, U., 9, 72
Development, 10; theory of, 10; model of, 10

Back Issue/Subscription Order Form

Copy or detach and send to:
Jossey-Bass Inc., Publishers, 350 Sansome Street, San Francisco CA 94104-1342

Call or fax toll free!
Phone 888-378-2537 6AM-5PM PST; Fax 800-605-2665

Back issues: Please send me the following issues at $23 each.
(Important: please include series initials and issue number, such as SS90.)

1. SS _____

_____

_____

$ _____ Total for single issues

$ _____ Shipping charges (for single issues *only;* subscriptions are exempt
from shipping charges): Up to $30, add $5^{50} • $30^{01}–$50, add $6^{50}
$50^{01}–$75, add $7^{50} • $75^{01}–$100, add $9 • $100^{01}–$150, add $10
Over $150, call for shipping charge.

Subscriptions   Please ❏ start   ❏ renew my subscription to *New Directions
for Student Services* for the year 19___ at the following rate:

     ❏ Individual $56   ❏ Institutional $99

NOTE: Subscriptions are quarterly, and are for the calendar year only.
Subscriptions begin with the spring issue of the year indicated above.
For shipping outside the U.S., please add $25.

$ _____ Total single issues and subscriptions (CA, IN, NJ, NY and DC
residents, add sales tax for single issues. NY and DC residents must
include shipping charges when calculating sales tax. NY and Canadian
residents only, add sales tax for subscriptions.)

❏ Payment enclosed (U.S. check or money order only)

❏ VISA, MC, AmEx, Discover Card #_____ Exp. date_____

Signature _____ Day phone _____

❏ Bill me (U.S. institutional orders only. Purchase order required.)

Purchase order #_____

Name _____

Address _____

_____

_____

Phone_____ E-mail _____

For more information about Jossey-Bass Publishers, visit our Web site at:
www.josseybass.com   **PRIORITY CODE = ND1**

OTHER TITLES AVAILABLE IN THE
NEW DIRECTIONS FOR STUDENT SERVICES SERIES
John H. Schuh, Editor-in-Chief
Elizabeth J. Whitt, Associate Editor